Published by John T. McFadden through Lulu Enterprises, Inc.

Morrisville, NC

ISBN: 978-0-6151-3773-5

Printed and Bound in the United States of America

BEAR SUIT FOLLIES

The songs, stories and letters of

ANTONIA

John T. McFadden, editor

Introduction

I first met Antonia in the fall of 1969 when I was a senior at Bucknell University in central Pennsylvania. I had been a rabid fan of the Holy Modal Rounders for years, even to the point of attempting to perform "Indian War Whoop" as a complete work at the local coffee house (it sounds more entertaining than it was). Susan and I were engaged at the time, with our wedding just a few months away. She claims that I courted her with Rounders music, and credits the longevity of our marriage in part to this (by which I think she means that she knew what she was getting into).

But I had never heard the Rounders perform live. In those pre-internet days, it was near impossible for folks outside of NYC (or wherever the Rounders, in part or in whole, were hanging out at a given time) to sort out what was going on with the band: two acoustic duo albums, long silence, bizarre acid-folk album, short silence, rumors of Eels…

Late that summer a friend living in Manhattan had stumbled upon a performance of a new incarnation of the Rounders, and came away with their manager's card. I made arrangements for the Rounders, whoever and whatever they now were, to play two shows on campus.

They arrived late, of course. Very late. The crowd that had jammed the room earlier was much reduced by the time the band finally set up. The first song they played was **CIA man** *("fuckin' A, CIA!")*. Amazingly, the older women working the counter at the student dive broke into big grins and started kicking their heels. The band was still a bit rough around the edges, but the energy was amazing.

5

Sitting immediately in front of the stage was a woman with the whitest hair I had ever seen, hair that almost glowed. She was holding the entire band fixed in an intense gaze while beating out the rhythms with two sticks of wood, keeping everyone on tempo. She struck me as a cross between a conductor leading an orchestra and a witch casting a spell, which I have since learned was exactly correct.

We had made arrangements for band members to spend the night with friends, a plan that quickly unraveled when various Rounders began to state their needs and preferences. Several, filled with back-to-the-land romanticism, wanted to be out in the country: Charlie and Mary took them out to the house they were renting from a Mennonite farmer. Two expressed a strong desire for a "needle friendly" environment, also not a problem in a college town in 1969. Which left Peter and Antonia. Antonia listed all the things to which she was allergic – an extensive list – and the only house that seemed to qualify was ours. I loaded them into my '61 Chevy ("oh me, hums like a bee...") and made up what passed for our guest bed. By morning we had been adopted into Antonia's extended family, a status we have enjoyed ever since. Notes and letters began to arrive with regularity, a stream of communication that has continued for 37 years.

We moved to New Jersey the following fall and remained there for 13 years, making many visits to Peter and Antonia (and later Antonia alone) in the celebrated rent-controlled apartment on West 55th Street. We accompanied Antonia to Rounders gigs at Folk City, the Bottom Line, and other clubs. When our children were born, she became their urban auntie, guiding them around her beloved Bronx Zoo, introducing them to the wonders of Italian street festivals, and escorting them to the best pizzeria in New York (they were mightily impressed that she carried her own pizza-cutter in her purse). From time to time she would take the bus out to visit us in Jersey, assaulting the buttoned-downed world of the "burbs" with her multi-hued muumuus and rhinestone-encrusted Minnie Mouse glasses. As I said, she was family.

Personal visits have been much less frequent since we moved to Wisconsin 23 years ago. The tide of letters has ebbed and flowed, with Antonia's health being a factor: there have been periods where even taking pen to paper has been more than she could manage. We continued to talk on the telephone with some regularity, but there were times when her voice was so weak that we strained to understand her. Still, there remained a strong sense of connection. Whenever the phone rings at "bear time," meaning just when we are about to go to bed and when Antonia's day is just getting rolling, we know whose voice we will hear when we answer.

In 2005 Antonia came very close to dying. She was living in an apartment in Sarasota and had not been managing her complex schedule of medications well. Likely there were issues with nutrition (never one of her strong suits) and hydration as well. She was taken to the hospital, followed by a long period of recuperation in a nursing home. For many months it was unclear whether she would need permanent care there. Her cousin and legal guardian, Geri (whom we have come to regard as heroic), schlepped back and forth between her home in Colorado and Sarasota, overseeing Antonia's care and trying to provide for the things most important to her quality of life (meaning getting out and about as often as possible; bears need to prowl).

It was during those months in the nursing home when her prospects for recovery were uncertain that I began to ponder collecting Antonia's writings into some sort of modest book. Her remarkable talent never earned her the audience she deserved, and it was tragic to think of her writings, her songs in particular, being forever lost.

How many songs has Antonia written? Not even Antonia knows for certain, but 200–300 would be a conservative estimate. How many of those songs still survive on record, demo tape, or scrap of notebook paper? How about her stories, pornographic and otherwise? Many of them appeared in publications that folded decades ago. And then there are the letters. I cannot guess how many we received in the course of nearly 40 years but we saved about 75. Did any of her other correspondents save her letters? I began making inquiries, and was immediately greeted with enthusiastic support and promises of help. Thus was born "the Antonia Project."

This has been very much a community effort, and it would not have been possible without the help of Geri Trochek (Antonia's cousin and legal guardian), Brendan Foreman, Maggie Roche, Corona, Kathryn Frederick and, of course, Peter Stampfel and Betsy Wollheim. Also, the whole gang from the "Have Moicy!" list (also informally called "the Rounders List") have offered invaluable support. Thanks, all!

INDEX

9

Chapter One: An Antonia Discography

"Indian War Whoop," The Holy Modal Rounders. (ESP 1068, 1967)

The third HMR record, generally credited with (or blamed for) the advent of "acid folk." Nobody had thought to apply electronic feedback to traditional music before. Stampfel and Weber are joined by playwright Sam Shepard on drums and Lee Crabtree on keyboards. Antonia can be heard (along with "Barbara" and "Wendy") singing, moaning, shrieking and yipping background vocals on several cuts (if the term "cuts" can even be applied to an album with no breaks between tracks, a clever design which, among other things, guaranteed that no song from this album could be cued up by a deejay). Antonia is credited as co-author (with Peter) of **Football Blues**, *which would be track three on side two, if the album had actual tracks.*

"The Moray Eels Eat the Holy Modal Rounders," The Holy Modal Rounders. (Elektra EKS-74026, 1968; CD re-release Water 101, 2002)

The most bizarre Rounders album of all? Some claim so. Producer Frazier Mohawk took many, shall we say,"liberties" with the tracks to shape them to his own (shall we be charitable?) "vision," although precisely what that vision was only Frazier knows. But because the universe has a sense of humor this album spawned the Rounders' – and Antonia's - one Big Hit Record when her **Bird Song** *was prominently featured on the soundtrack of the film* **Easy Rider**. *The album also contains three songs credited to Antonia and Peter:* **Take-off Artist Song, Mobile Line Gonna Take Me Away from the Curse of the Bullfrog Blues,** *and* **The Duji Song**.

11

"Good Taste is Timeless," The Holy Modal Rounders. (Metromedia Records MD1039, 1971; CD re-release Sundazed SC6208, 2003)

The Rounders, now a genuine six-member band, recorded this one in Nashville. Antonia is co-credited (with Weber and Stampfel) for **Black Bottom Blues** *and, with Peter, for the hysterically funny* **Livin' Off the Land**.

"Alleged in their Own Time," The Holy Modal Rounders. (Rounder Records 3004, 1975)

Back to mostly acoustic music, with Luke Faust and Robin Remaily joining Stampfel and Weber for this one. The album included an eight-page insert of liner notes which featured Peter and Antonia's delightful (and thoroughly pornographic) short story, "Wicked Arabella." The nice folks at the Rounder Collective (they named their label in honor of the HMR) felt compelled to post a discrete warning label warning sensitive souls that the notes carried an "X" rating, this long before the age of MPAA warnings. The only topic not covered in these eight pages of notes (mostly rambling discourse from Peter at his best) is any information about the songs and their authorship. But Antonia wrote **Low Down Dog** *(verses added by Weber and Remaily). She and Peter co-wrote* **Synergy,** *and* **Voodoo Queen Marie** *is one of her most celebrated set of lyrics, set to an old-timey melody. It is the only recorded song on which Antonia sings lead vocal. Sadly, it is presently out of print.*

"Have Moicy!" Michael Hurley, the Unholy Modal Rounders, Jeffery Frederick and the Clamtones. (Rounder Records 3010, 1976; CD reissue 1991)

The West Coast Rounders and the East Coast Rounders (a/k/a the Unholies) join forces with Hurley and the Clamtones – the whole, mad extended family – to make one of the great albums of all times. Featured on a number of "albums of the year" and "best albums of all times" lists, it introduced Rounders music, previously confined to a limited but appreciative audience to, well, a slightly larger limited audience. "Have Moicy" includes two of Antonia's signature songs, both incredibly infectious: **Griselda** *and* **Hoodoo Bash***. Also on this album is her collaboration with Paul Presti,* **Jealous Daddy's Death Song***.*

"Last Round," The Holy Modal Rounders. (Adelphi 1030, 1978; CD reissue 2000)

Another collaborative project of sorts, with Peter and Weber joining forces with the Rounders/Clamtones (which counted HMR stalwarts Richard Tyler, Dave Reisch, and Robin Remaily as members at the time; it is all quite incestuous). This time the insert was only six pages in length and contained the even dirtier Peter/Antonia story, "Marybeth's Dreadful Ordeal." Except it really wasn't really an insert because you had to send away for it. Songs by Antonia include **That Belly I Idolize** *(co-authored with Peter; Weber sings it well but drops half of her verses), a de-Fraziered version of* **Bird Song***, the joyously vulgar* **Snappin' Pussy***, and the haunting* **God, What Am I Doing Here?**

13

"Going Nowhere Fast," The Holy Modal Rounders. (Rounder Records 3051, 1981)

Peter and Weber perform as an acoustic duo on record for the first time since 1965, no easy task given that by this time getting a performance out of Weber was more challenging that luring Brian Wilson out of his sandbox. It includes two of Antonia's most beautiful songs, **Jeanine's Dream** *and* **Dance in Slow Motion**, *whose lyrics she set to the waltz tune "Spanish Fandango," a standard guitar piece in the late nineteenth century. The album also contains Antonia's only known collaboration with William Shakespeare,* **Lovin' Mad Tom** *(her tune, his words).*

"Peter Stampfel and the BottleCaps," Peter Stampfel and the Bottlecaps. (Rounder Records 9003, 1986)

The first album by Peter's post-Rounders band, featuring guitarist John Scherman (with whom he had been playing and performing for two years) featured five songs on which Antonia collaborated: **Surfer Angel** *(Peter, J. Scherman, Antonia),* **Random Violence** *(Daisanne McLean, Peter and Antonia),* **Lonely Junkie** *(Peter and Antonia),* **Everything Must Go** *(J. Scherman, Peter, and Antonia), and* **Funny the First Time** *(J. Scherman, Peter and Antonia).* **Random Violence** *and* **Lonely Junkie** *manage to be both very funny and profoundly disturbing at the same time, which is not an easy trick.*

14

"The People's Republic of Rock and Roll," Peter Stampfel and the Bottlecaps. (Homestead Records 133-4, 1989)

The second Bottlecaps release includes one of the many songs Antonia coauthored with Mark Johnson, **When Things Come True***, along with* **Mindless Boogie** *(J. Scherman/Antonia), and* **New York Minute** *(J. Scherman/Antonia).*

"Fakebook," Yo Le Tenga. (Bar/None Records, 1990)

This comparatively "mainstream" album contains a wonderful version of **Griselda***.*

"12 in a room," Mark Johnson. (1992, CD rerelease Radioghost Records/Applehead Records, 2005)

Mark's much-acclaimed "underground classic" album includes three of the many songs he coauthored with Antonia, **Earn That Love**, **Desperate***,* and **I like the World***.*

"Not in our Wildest Dreams…," Peter Stampfel/The Dysfunctionells. (rockink, 1995)

The Dysfunctionells were reputedly formed around a common obsession with HMR music, and Peter's contribution to it in particular: This is a collection of live performances in Chicago and New York in which they performed with their musical inspiration. Many HMR chestnuts are revisited, including **Griselda** *and* **Hoodoo Bash**.

"Too Much Fun!" The Holy Modal Rounders. (Rounder CD 3163, 1999)

Back together yet once more: the original Stampfel and Weber performing acoustically, with help from Dave Reisch. Even Frazier Mohawk is back! World peace may be possible after all! Connoisseurs rank this one with their very best work, and it includes a never-previously recorded Stampfel/Antonia collaboration, **Bad Boy***, based on a girl-group recording of a song based on "Stagolee."*

"Freak Mountain Ramblers," The Freak Mountain Ramblers. (1999)

Spiritual and musical heirs to the Rounders/Clamtones in the Portland area, the FMRs count Dave Reisch as a member, and he arranged the version of **That Belly I idolize** *that appears on this, their first album.*

"No Knowledge of Music Required," The Du-Tels. (Shimmy Disc 5103, 2000)

The band Peter formed with Gary Lucas. Includes a new rendition of **Voodoo Queen Marie***, this time credited to Peter and Antonia rather than Antonia alone, which is likely correct.*

Last Night on the Roller Coaster," Mark Johnson. (Radioghost Records, 2000)

This album includes four songs written by Antonia and Mark, **Drifting***,* **Eyes***,* **Those Pretty Things***, and* **Rhythm of the World***.*

"I Make a Wish for a Potato," The Holy Modal Rounders and Friends. (Rounder Records 3719, 2001)

A compilation album with tracks from various records, some still in print and others long unavailable, it brings the "Have Moicy" gang back on the stage for a final bow. Songs by Antonia included here are **Low Down Dog***,* **Bad Boy***, and* **Synergy***.*

"Bird Song: Live 1971," The Holy Modal Rounders. (Water Records 1HN5CM, 2004)

This live performance of the Rounders in transition to "good-time jam band" includes versions of **Low Down Dog** *and* **Bird Song**.

"The Cicada and Other Stories," Bingo. (Cravedog Records, 2004)

Bingo (Kevin Richey), ex-member of Golden Delicious and sometime Freak Mountain Rambler, includes his version of **God, What am I doing Here?** *on this, his third solo record.*

"The Holy Modal Rounders B.C.," Steve Weber. (Frederick Productions CDFP006, 2006).

This live recording of Weber and the West Coast Rounders includes versions of **Black Bottom Blues**, ***Bird Song***, *and* ***Low Down Dog***.

"Jeffrey Frederick's Clamtones B.C." (Frederick Productions CDFP004, 2006)

Two-disc set from the same Vancouver gig includes a version of ***Griselda***.

"The Jig is Up," Peter Stampfel and the Bottlecaps. (Blue Navigator CRR381, 2006)

This "enhanced disc" (includes a video of "Bridge and Tunnel Girls"!) features the only recording of **Running Pissing Man**, *Peter's words set to Antonia's tune, as well as* **Freddy's Blues**.

"Antonia's 11," Peter Stampfel. (Blue Navigator, 2006).

This album was recorded for the "Special Antonia issue" of the publication **Blue Navigator** *which has a primary focus on the music of Michael Hurley. The album is available only with that issue. It includes eleven songs, only one of which has previously been recorded, beginning with the infamous* **Fucking Sailors in Chinatown**. *The others are* **New Happy Time, Nightwalking, New Limehouse Blues, Places Where You Never See the Snow, Laura the Horse, Freddy's Blues, Sentimental Song, Cajun Polka, Float Me Down Your Pipeline,** *and (at long last!)* **Going to See the King**.

Chapter Two: Essays, Interviews, and Remembrances of Antonia

A Few Layers of the Antonia Onion

John McFadden

In pulling together these writings and other materials it was certainly not my intention to write a biography of Antonia, much less a history of the Holy Modal Rounders. But I have been necessarily plunged deeply into her life, and the Rounders story, in the course of this project. Antonia is a deep, wise and complicated lady, and the Rounders history in which she played such an integral role has taken such convoluted twists and turns that only those who participated in them along the way have any hope of keeping them straight.

Susan and I were at the periphery of most of these events. We were appropriating many of them second-hand, through Antonia's letters and phone calls. In his essay on Antonia, Peter describes her as "sneaky" (in a good way). Perhaps one manifestation of that sneakiness is what she chose to emphasize or deemphasize with various people in her world. Susan and I were among the very limited number of comparatively "straight" people in that world (most of the others were her family members). I am a clergyman and Susan is a university professor. Through many years of our friendship with Antonia we were also the parents of young children. Antonia did not in any way attempt to hide things like her porn (she was too proud of it) or drug use from us, but neither did she dwell on them. We saw the goodness, the kindness, the deep intellect, the wisdom, and the remarkable creative talent. We were grateful to be accepted for who and what we were, and we accepted Antonia as she was in return.

∎∎∎

Antonia grew up in Greenpoint in Brooklyn as Barbara Ann Goldblatt. It was largely a community of second-generation immigrants (Irish, Italian, Polish) establishing themselves in the emerging middle class. Antonia's father was Jewish (not common in Greenpoint), her mother Polish. She was a scary-brilliant girl, living in the tension many bright girls from good families do: an angel on one shoulder and a devil on the other. She read voraciously, science fiction in particular (back when the genre was still in its golden age of mind-expanding brilliance). She was writing poems, songs and stories as soon as she learned to read. She was a born story-teller: she would read her stories in front of her class and bask in the glow of the attention.

By the time she reached junior high she was thoroughly immersed in popular music, and being a Brooklyn girl this meant doo-wop in particular, doing arrangements for a vocal group (*"Touch and the Untouchables"*) formed by some of her friends. She was a bright girl from a good household, but was drawn towards the other side of the figurative tracks; she discovered the joys of being a bad girl early and never looked back. She still describes herself as a "sexual outlaw," and for her this is a proud and defining claim.

Antonia gave birth to a child when she was sixteen. This was an era where respectable, middle-class girls did not become pregnant; rather they disappeared for the better part of a school year because they were (the Goldblatts' official explanation) "visiting a cousin in Florida." In reality the family moved to Queens, where Antonia had the baby and gave her up for adoption. Bright as she was, she barely missed a beat in her schooling, graduating on time.

She enrolled in drama school, not because she wanted to be a professional actress but because she saw it as a means to journey deeply within. Drama school pulled her into the emerging Bohemian/beat scene in New York: black clothing, poetry, jazz and, inevitably, drugs. This would have been around 1959.

Like many bright and curious people, she read Huxley's *Doors of Perception* and had the immediate reaction "Where can I get some of this stuff?" She was a psychedelic pioneer, expanding (distorting, if you prefer) her consciousness with various hallucinogens many years before *Time* and *Newsweek* alerted the culture at large that such things existed. Consciousness-expansion in this era was an intellectual and spiritual endeavor, and Antonia was a high priestess in this world of hallucinogens, instructing others as a psychedelic guide.

New York being New York, Bohemian intellectuals experimenting with psychedelics were bound to intersect with the well-established "hard drug" world of heroin and methamphetamines. In his essay *Ten Years Ago in Greenwich Village*, Peter Stampfel offers a glimpse of the emerging coffee house/folk music scene in the very early sixties. Those of us who discovered folk music a few years later – say '63 or '64 – were titillated at the thought that some of the musicians might occasionally puff on a reefer. In the Village, hard drugs had already been deeply interwoven with the musical culture for years. The first two Holy Modal Rounder albums, cut in '63 and '64, struck most listeners as filled with a kind of innocent, irreverent exuberance, but Stampfel and Weber were heavily fueled by meth as well as pot when they recorded them.

Which is to say that by the time hippie culture blossomed in all its tie-dyed glory, marijuana and psychedelics were last year's news among New York's musical cognoscenti. There was virtually no one in Antonia's universe who did not use drugs, heavily and frequently. "Bad" drug users were those so profoundly addicted (most commonly to heroin) that they were untrustworthy, unreliable, and dishonest. "Good" drug users did not rip off their friends, rob their apartments, or slide all the way down the sinkhole of self-destruction.

Antonia knew a fair number of the former, and most everyone else she knew, including herself, was one of the latter.

Methamphetamine became her drug of choice, and remained so for decades. Meth fit well with her pattern of howling and prowling all night, and provided energy for her frequent bursts of creative writing. It was not uncommon for her to keep going, fueled by speed, for several days and nights before crashing. "Speed Queen" was one of her chosen alter egos, and she more than lived up to it.

In all the years of our friendship, I never saw Antonia obviously impaired. As some of the letters I include suggest, as her health deteriorated the speed became a kind of self-medication needed just to function "normally." She has suffered for many years from tardive dyskonesia, a nasty condition that was likely worsened by physicians who kept her on very strong medications for far too long. Using speed actually provided relief from some of her symptoms, a classic "damned if you do and damned if you don't" choice. But she also just really liked the stuff.

Only occasionally did I get a glimpse of how important speed was to Antonia. One afternoon I took a friend to visit Peter and Antonia. He was then a graduate student at the University of Minnesota, where he had stumbled across a paper bag containing several ounces of marijuana, many tabs of acid, and a vial of unknown powder while walking through a park, a pretty exciting discovery in 1971. He told the story to Peter and Antonia, who asked about the powder. He was carrying it with him, not really sure what to do with an unknown substance (speed? coke? drain cleaner?). Antonia whipped out a straw and, to my amazement, assessed the powder (speed, as it turned out) like a wine expert evaluating a fine burgundy. Speed Queen indeed.

There is no question but that long-term use of amphetamines played a significant role in the deterioration of Antonia's health, and is at least partially responsible for her residing in an assisted-living facility at the age of 67. Certainly she knows this, but has never expressed regret about this or anything else (other than her mild regret that she once refused to have sex with Bob Dylan because "he had the worst beer breath!"). Without the speed, she would not have been Antonia, would not have lived the life she lived, would – in all likelihood – not have produced the body of wonderful work she did.

▪▪

The story of how she brought Weber and Stampfel together to form the Holy Modal Rounders is told elsewhere in this collection. But I hope I am not crossing any boundaries by sharing a few thoughts on her relationship with Peter. She was, by the way, briefly married in the early sixties, which is why you will sometimes stumble across the name "Antonia Duren." I know nothing about that marriage, and it does not seem to have any real bearing on her story. During her psychedelic guide/musical muse days she was known simply as "Antonia." After living with Peter for many years in what amounted to a common-law marriage, she took the name "Stampfel" and uses it to this day.

To steal a title from one of their songs, their relationship was defined by a remarkable creative synergy. They taught and learned from one another. Both were collectors, each was unable to be "moderately interested" in any topic; both were, and are, people of passion and great enthusiasm. Peter, for example, is well-known for his collection of vintage bottle-caps, but it is less widely known that he has what is undoubtedly the world's most extensive collection of post-war Milwaukee bus transfers (they truly are amazing). They both loved science fiction and fantasy. Add Antonia's fascination with witchcraft and (later) her fixation on all things Star Trek. A simply amazing amount of Stuff was somehow crammed into that little apartment.

There was a period of several years, spanning the late sixties and early seventies, where they were so thoroughly in sync with one another that they could write a lengthy story like "MaryBeth's Dreadful Ordeal" in tag-team shifts, with no discernable change in voice along the way. Many of the songs they co-authored during this period are among their very best, and they are collaborations in the truest sense, almost the product of a common mind.

But there was a darker side to those years, including growing dependence on drugs. In his liner notes for the CD re-release of "the Moray Eels Eat the Holy Modal Rounders," Richie Unterberger describes how spooked Frazier Mohawk was when he visited Peter and Antonia in their apartment and was forced to sit in silence while they demonstrated their ability to predict –often accurately – the next song that would play on the radio. Magic, sex, and rock & roll were all cooking together in a big vat of speed, which is not a formula for good physical or mental health.

Which brings us to the Peter/Betsy/Antonia triangle. Betsy had already known Peter for many years, carrying what some would describe as a long-term crush. Through the mid-seventies she became closer to both Peter and Antonia, moving Antonia to describe her frequently as "my best friend." This makes it easy to set up a tale of "he done me wrong" betrayal. Given that the "Rounders community" is an opinionated bunch, not greatly enamored with minding its own collective business, there certainly were any number of people ready to describe events in those terms: of Peter abandoning a woman in failing health for a young, vital, and affluent woman; of the woman who "stole" his affections while pretending to be Antonia's friend.

My perspective (and I speak only for myself) is that if Peter and Antonia had continued on the path they were on they would have both vanished down the sinkhole of self-destruction decades ago. I cherish Betsy. When we first met, my first thought was (please remember that we were the "straight" folks visiting Planet Rounders) "she's a member of my tribe!" Betsy is firm, clear, disciplined; in Antonia's words a "whip-cracker" (and she says that as a compliment, recognizing that Peter needed a whip-cracker and that she could never be that).

When Peter married Betsy his world became a far healthier place. They are now the parents of two wonderful young women. He has been straight and sober for years. He has maintained his musical output, and I believe he would say it has improved as well (opinionated Rounders fans of course hold their various opinionated opinions on that). He has continued to pursue his role as a major American musicologist (there are times when I think this may prove to be his greatest contribution and legacy). It will never be simple, or easy, to be Peter Stampfel, but without Betsy I shudder to imagine what he would be like today, if he would be at all.

And Antonia? She was inspired – forced, perhaps – to develop coping skills and strategies. She discovered new and gifted collaborators to work with musically, notably Mark Johnson, while continuing to work with Peter. She formed new networks of friends and developed new interests. She reconnected with her own family, including her cousin, Geri. She grew deeper and wiser, coping with adversity and loss with grace, humor, and compassion for others. She learned the practice of aging with flair, creativity, and Attitude. She became increasingly grateful for small things, demonstrating remarkable resilience and courage.

Did she get the short end of the stick? Certainly she did in financial terms (although Peter continues to provide financial support, and friendship, to this day). But I return to where I began: Together they gave the world musical gifts that neither could have given alone. For that we should all be grateful. But had they stayed together, they would have likely carried one another down a spiral of destructiveness.

I mentioned earlier the amazing amount of Stuff in the apartment where Antonia had lived since 1969. Presumably half the Stuff in there was Peter's yet, amazingly, when he moved out there was no less Stuff. His current loft includes the "dreaded spare room" that is absolutely crammed with Stuff, and I know that much of it came from the old apartment; I can only theorize that Antonia's Stuff immediately doubled in volume as soon as Peter's Stuff vacated the space.

When Antonia moved to Florida she left her winter clothing and (at least according to her) most of her Stuff behind, yet her new apartment, the same size as the New York one, was soon completely filled with Stuff. This gal defies normal laws of physics.

The reason she has so much Stuff is because she has so many interests, and she has a very hard time parting with anything associated with those interests. When we are deeply interested in a topic, we refer to it as a "passion." When someone else is deeply interested in a topic, we label it an "obsession." Whichever term you choose, Antonia has it in spades. Bears of all types have been a major focus of her passion (hence her best-known alter ego of "Singing Bear"): for many years we received an annual card from Antonia celebrating "New Bears Eve," the night when all the world's bears are reputedly born en masse. In recent decades, her two most abiding passions have been Star Trek and birds. I know a very little about the former, virtually nothing about the latter, but this has in no way discouraged Antonia from sharing these passions with me. When you love someone, you accept their passions as a part of who they are (although you do try to shift the topic every once in awhile).

She has a remarkable ability to blend her passions in odd and intriguing ways. For example, "porn" and "Star Trek" are not topics most of us would think to associate with one another or use in the same sentence, but leave it to Antonia. She owns what must surely be one of the world's largest collections of a literary sub-genre fondly referred to by its fans as "slash." Slash, as in Kirk/Spock: fanzines predicated on the idea that Captain Kirk and Mr. Spock shared more than a professional working relationship. Oddly, these stories are written and read almost entirely by women.

When I visited Antonia last September, she worked up the courage to make an unusual request. There was a box beneath her bed that she was too weak to pull out. In that box were some of her favorite "slash" books. Others were still at her apartment. Her cousin Geri was coming in a few days to clear out her apartment. Since her small room at the assisted-living facility already contained more Stuff than it should have been able to contain, she and Geri would need to engage in "Stuff triage." Could I pull the box out and review the "slash" so she could sort out which books were where?

So the Bear and I spent an evening curled up on her bed as other residents pushed their walkers down the hallway outside, reading about the sexual escapades of Kirk and Spock. Several nights later, at a trendy restaurant on St. Armand's Circle, sitting with Geri and her husband Matt, I encouraged her to raise the topic of how she could fit more "slash" into her small room. Geri, fellow member of my "straight people tribe," glanced at me, the minister, with something like alarm. "You know about the **slash**?" You bet, Geri.

I love this woman dearly, and have learned much from her through the years, including a great deal about courage and strength. I hope and pray that the Bear has many good and rich years left in her, and that we will enjoy her friendship for a long time to come.

But as I ponder my own process of aging and what it may bring, I am heartened by the image of an assisted-living facility in Florida where there resides a brilliant, musically-gifted sexual outlaw. She is gracious, kind and polite. She makes few demands and tries to be helpful to others. But she has her secrets and she has her stories. And she has a box of filthy books carefully hidden beneath her bed.

TEN YEARS AGO IN GREENWICH VILLAGE: A DISJOINTED HISTORY OF THE EARLY COFFEE HOUSE FOLK SCENE

Peter Stampfel (originally published in *Crawdaddy*, circa 1971)

The italicized section in the middle of this essay was written by Antonia. She participated in the "interesting evening" she describes.

It all started on the Lower East Side, now the East village, during the Second World War. Woody Guthrie, Leadbelly and Pete Seeger were living on East 10th Street. All through the forties. Infusing the area with the heaviest folk karma. All I know about that scene is from a friend who was there then.

"What happened?" I asked.

"Woody's old lady ran off with a sailor," he said.

Then Tom Paley came to town. Tom Paley is one nifty dude. More than anyone else, perhaps, he introduced the modern acoustic guitar and banjo-picking styles to New York. Before Paley, nearly everybody except the 10th St. vanguard thrashed grossly on the nylon stringed guitar. Paley brought Travis and Scruggs to the Big Apple, clear as a bell.

In 1953, Folkways Records released the Harry Smith *Anthology of American Folk Music*, and a mighty release it was too. 84 cuts of Mississippi John Hurt, the Carter Family, Charlie Poole, Blind Lemon Jefferson, Uncle Dave Macon, the Memphis Jug Band, Blind Willie Johnson, Eck Robertson, shape-note hymns, cajun music – a six record set, released just before rhythm and blues became pop. The lot of them were recorded between 1927 and 1931. The Harry Smith anthology is where I and thousands of others learned about country music, Cajun music, etc.

The way that I started getting money for playing music was that two of my old friends had jobs at this Jewish home for girls who had been committed to a posh flip house called Hillside. The girls were able to get out of Hillside by living in this Jewish Home in Brooklyn and observing curfew, etc. I had been reading trilogies and learning to play the fiddle in an effort to ease my heart, which had recently been broken by a young lady from Queens. It was early 1960, and I was living on the Lower East Side. I picked it up pretty fast and so my friends invited me to join the group.

The social function we were to brighten was the dreaded once-a-year Visit of mommies and daddies to see their wayward daughters. Boy, it sure was an uptight scene.

We were Mac Grundy's Old Timey Wool Thumpers and we played old-timey music. Wool thumping is an old-timey expression for sexual congress – quaint, ain't it? The girls really liked us, and everybody else there really hated us....but we were gonna get them with this real nifty routine we had worked out in the middle of this instrumental piece called 'Dallas Rag.' See, it had this 3 beat pause; on the first beat I, standing in the middle, ducked down, on the second beat George Dawson knocked the corncob pipe out of Rob Hunter's mouth, and on the third beat I stood up again, so that we were able to resume playing on the fourth beat. We practiced that bit very hard. The big moment comes. I duck down, Dawson swings... and connects. The pipe goes flying, straight as an arrow, towards this scowling old dyke who is head of the home and hates us because we got long hair and dress funny and play this music. Bonk! The corn-cob pipe hits her smack dab in the middle of her forehead. "Gasp," go all the mommies and daddies in perfect unison. Hunter and Dawson collapse to the floor in compulsive laughter. I'm in the middle, still playing my mandolin, and kicking each of them in turn so they'll get up and help me finish. Blood trickles out of the corner of my mouth because I'm biting my tongue to keep from laughing. Well, we finished together, but they only paid us fifteen dollars instead of thirty. Whatta debut!

At that time, I didn't know what the Village folk scene was like apart from what happened at the Folklore Centre because I believed the Village was full of phonies and that the real people all lived on the Lower East Side. Dumb snobbery on my part.

Anyway, I went to California for a year and made the amazing discovery that I could play music in coffee houses and get paid for it. In late summer 1961, I got back to New York and moved to a place on MacDougall Street, across from the Cafe Wha'. Making the rounds of the folk haunts, I discovered that most of the people playing there were cruddier than me. I'd been considering myself as not a nifty enough musician to make it in New York, but hell, I was plenty nifty enough. The Beat Generation movement was on, and the scene was coffee houses – and in many of these places you weren't paid, but passed a hat to the annoyed tourists who were already put out by the bad overpriced coffee. Folk and flamenco got played, and poetry got read, but nobody who was anybody admitted to liking rock'n'roll. The local heroes were Fred Neil, Dino Valente and Bob Dylan. Dino had this flair for the dramatic even then, and he used to get put down by the dedicated and professional folkies for changing chords and words to make old songs sound more dramatic. His changes added a lot to the emotional impact of the songs, and the crowds loved it – and he could really get you hopping up and down in your seat with his train rhythm songs. I remember, one morning, he and Karen Dalton were wailing out a high-voltage version of 'Chickens they are crowing', and at about 4 am, an annoyed neighbor came down and kicked in the glass door of the cafe. Dino was ready to kill him. So was I... I could have listened to that song all night. The basket-passing coffee houses had no legal entertainment licenses, and there was a lot of bad feeling between the old residents of Greenwich Village and the musicians who came in looking to sing and play. We musicians kept musicians' hours (noon to four in the morning) and the older straight people were resentful; they kept trying to close the cafes down and get all the Undesirables out of the Village. But we just went on making music, listening to it, avoiding dark alleys, and eating potburgers at dawn when we usually all went to someone's house after we'd done our evening's and night's work. Then we would all go up on the roof and listen to Dino as he sang and played the sun up.

It was the time of the crystal. Hallucinogens had just cracked on the scene, and I lost my atheism unexpectedly when I came face to face with the reality of God's existence. When I was straight again, God was still there, so I accepted it. I mean, fighting it is a lost cause. I well remember the first batch of acid coming into New York. The guy who had it put it onto 200 sugar cubes, then he took the sugar to the Village, from coffee house to coffee house, handing it out to everybody he found performing there. The circuit took him two hours to complete, and then he went back to the first place he'd visited and made his rounds again, this time observing the results of his handiwork. It was certainly an interesting evening.

Fred Neil's haunting voice and fatal charm were elements that colored the scene; even then, he had that incredible beauty of note-choices and purple-blue shading of tones that characterizes his singing. He is one of the best singers around, and everybody wanted to be Fred in those days. Then Tim Hardin arrived in town, bringing his ghosts and his graceful, shimmering music – but he always seemed to be on the point of leaving for somewhere, even when he'd only just arrived. The streets filled up with fifteen year old girls in peasant dresses. Richie Havens began to get noticed, starting out in the basket-passing cafes, but soon proving that he could hold and sway an audience in the paying clubs. Competition to get into the few paying clubs was keen; you had to be able to hold an audience, and that meant you had to have a style and sound of your own – and Richie had that. He too reworked old tunes, but he also had this tremendous ability to involve the audience in his songs. He is modest and genuinely friendly, seeking to share something with his audience rather than show off – and the audience senses this and in turn responds warmly.

In the summer of '61, things really began to cook. Up to that time, about the only person playing traditional type stuff and making it work for people who were not into traditional music was Dave Van Ronk. Dave taught a lot of people how to play guitar and several thousand guitarists play his classically traditional arrangements. Precious few of this group, however, have Van Ronk's taste, phrasing, balls and sense of style. Most of the traditionally-oriented musicians were into very technical trips – Perry Lederman was one of the few around who could bring it off. Back in those benighted times, the hip Jewish kids were into bluegrass and had been since at least the mid 50s. The blues and traditional thing came later.

The reason that things started to cook in that summer of '61 was the arrival of Ramblin' Jack Elliott and Bob Dylan, from across the Atlantic and from the mid-west respectively. Ramblin' Jack immediately blew everybody's mind with his flawless taste and his ability never to play too much guitar, but the right guitar to back his singing.

1 first saw Dylan in a coffee house that successively changed its name from the Commons to the Fat Black Pussycat to the Feenjon. 1 assumed he was a punk motorcycle type because he wore this punk motorcycle type hat. He was 20, and just about beardless – you know, he looked like that photo of him on his first album. I missed him the first time he played at Gerde's Folk City, although I saw him from outside, playing away; I couldn't hear him, but he didn't look like a motorcycle punk when he moved with that guitar. I heard him play a little later, and talk about having your mind blown... that same incredible rush as when I heard Little Richard for the first time, in 1956. He started his set with a fiddly-banjo type tune called 'Sally Ann,' which just about took the top of my head off. He was doing all traditional songs, but it was his approach! His singing style and phrasing were stone rhythm and blues – he fitted the two styles together perfectly, clear as a bell, and I realized for the first time that my two true loves, traditional music and rock music, were in fact one. They were one!

As winter settled into 1961, I got a really ace job at the Gaslight Cafe, just a two minute walk from where I lived. The manager was going to try something new; traditional music all through the winter – he figured the time was right to get a lot of people interested in it. I got 75 dollars a week, plus another 25 for announcing who was on next, and I was supposed to be their resident singer for the whole of the winter.

The first two weeks, I worked with Dylan and Jim Kweskin. They did a lot of stuff together, including the definitive version of 'San Francisco Bay

Blues'... they sure were dynamite. Dylan didn't like having to play twice every night, so he quit after two weeks.

One thing about Dylan – make that two things. First, a valuable thing he gave me; I had just turned 23 and was hitting the point where it was easy to look down on people 5 or so years younger. It was a lot easier to do back then, because damn few people under 21 could do anything at all original. Perry Lederman, again, was one of the exceptions, his style being at once super-flashy and super-technical, yet super-ballsy too. Anyway, here was Dylan, just 20, and doing something that nobody at any age was doing better. By 1966 it wasn't uncommon for people between, say, 14 and 20 to be into excellent original stuff, but in 1961 it was rare. Anyway, before Dylan, I often pre-judged people unfairly on the basis of age. After Dylan, I didn't. The other thing about him was his brilliant ability to communicate to an audience but his inability to deal effectively with people on a one-to-one basis. He sometimes misinterpreted the actions of those around him and this was one of the only characteristics he had which could be referred to as flawed – though he was in one hell of a better shape than I ever was at 20. Anyway, this "flaw" was just a growing pain that he'd got over by the time he achieved a wide popularity.

Another thing that surprises me about Dylan is how long it took people to hear his voice. People who heard him back then often go on about how bad he used to sound; he sounded great then, it just took them a long time to learn how to listen.

In the winter of 61/62, the Gaslight featured Dylan, Kweskin, me, Sandy Bull, Luke Faust, Dave Ray (who'd been washing dishes at the Fat Black

Pussycat) and Jack Elliott, and people like Ian & Sylvia would often drop in later on, after they'd finished working at the Blue Angel uptown.

Summer '62 was a busy summer. Four years earlier, the folk music/coffee house beatnik tie-up had originated, but in 1962 the above syndrome was securely hooked up to the protest and drug movements....everybody was taking acid and talking about it at length; you could hardly start a conversation without talking about drugs.

This may sound hard to believe, but all everybody in folk music talked about from summer '62 until Kennedy's death fifteen months later, was drugs. Some other things that happened during that summer are: people started hitting you for spare change on the streets (ugh) and 12 year old runaways started hanging around the Village for the first time. Many new words sprang up and got popular in the community – like "uptight," "old man," "old lady", "spaced," "boxed," "rap" and "needle-freak!" 1962 also brought speed, with the resulting amphetamine guitar style. Speedfreaks were called "A-heads" back then.

That summer also brought John Sebastian and Phil Ochs to the Village and around this time too, people started to hang out in the Nite Owl. The prior favorite hangout place was the Fat Black Pussycat, then the Nite Owl started to take over – at first, because it was so unhip... I mean, wall-to-wall Keane paintings indeed! But a lot of hookers hung out there and it was also pretty hip to know a lot of hookers in 1962.

1963 brought morning glory seeds and the news that Mississippi John Hurt had been rediscovered. It also brought the Holy Modal Rounders (Stampfel and Steve Weber) to the basket-passing world of the Village. By then,

Weber had set a heap of styles – he was the first to wear Ben Franklin style shades, was the first cat I ever saw with Afro-style Helix hair, and he also established the world record for walking barefoot in New York without getting one's foot cut – an amazing seven months.

Oh yeah, the other big number from 1962 was the pot shortage, which lasted the summer long. This was simply a result of unprecedented numbers of people starting to use it, and there wasn't sufficient to go round. As people explained at the time, pot went uptown. There was a hallucinogen shortage too, for the same reason, and this went on well into '63.

Bleecker Street and MacDougall on a Friday night: carnage, pillage, everyone uptight, I only go to meet my friends or score.

Just one more thing about 1962; that was the year when the Beatles, Stones, Dylan, the Beach Boys, etc. began to get established on a popular level; in short, rock music became hip that year. Just as Dylan put poetry and music back together, the Beatles and the Stones put popular culture and art back together. In those 'good old days' everybody in the Village would say "It's bad enough to sell", and this, of course, rationalized their own failures. This kind of nonsense is what the Beatles killed.... not folk music.

Antonia

Peter Stampfel (*courtesy of **Blue Navigator***)

Since she invented the Holy Modal Rounders, it surely all started with Antonia. But where, musically, did she begin, and how did she manage to even qualify for concocting such an odd musical fabrication? Rather, who else on the planet could have possibly conceived of Weber and I playing together? Look, here's what she did – regularly – to the Star Spangled Banner in High School:

She would start by singing just a little sharp, or a little flat, and either a little behind the beat, or ahead of it. By the time said banner was being proudly hailed at the twilight's last gleaming, an ever-growing circle with Antonia (who was then still Barbara Ann Goldblatt, but that's another story) in the middle, was solidly off pitch and rhythm. Some voices would try to correct, as the proper version was still quite audible, but by the time the ramparts were being watched over, a sizable amount of the auditorium was firmly lost and in several dozen different places. The cascade of chaos by now was going full tilt. And while bombs and rockets were proving that the flag was still there, the song was disintegrating into utter musical Babel. Each and every time it disintegrated totally before they even got to the land of the free and the home of the brave. Although in a way, thanks to Antonia, that's where everyone was.

Sheer musical genius.

I was born in 1938. Antonia was born in 1939. When we were twelve years old, we each bought our first record – Gershwin's Rhapsody in Blue.

Being in Brooklyn, (Greenpoint) Antonia heard r&b years before I did, and while in High School in the mid 50s, she was a member and arranger for a doo-wop group called Touch and the Untouchables. Touch was a James Deanish looking Brooklyn kid who would carry lost pups and kittens inside his leather jacket. He sang lead. Antonia showed the backup guys their background "Ooooos", bob-she-bops, etc. She favored parallel fourths and fifths. She then did the "high screaming" parts – the equivalent of lead guitar. They broke up when high school was over. Of course, they never recorded.

But she didn't know anything about country blues until she met Weber in the early '60s. He proceeded to educate her by playing specific records to get specific points across. He would play a cut once, or dozens of times, however many times it took until Antonia got whatever musical nuance he was trying to convey (by this time, she was Antonia). He would never spell out what the particular "lesson" was for a given cut. He would never ask if she got it, nor would she say now I do. But he would always know when she had, and wouldn't repeat the cut. Every time. Clearly, the Rounder telepathy predates the Rounders.

Antonia and Weber had a lot of fights. One of the most frequent was about Weber's insistence that only he was real, and the rest of the world didn't exist. Antonia would refute this, but Weber wasn't buying any. Antonia finally won the argument by breaking Weber's guitar over his head. They broke up in 1962.

Antonia wrote a number of unrecorded songs about her relationship with Weber. Here's one:

Sentimental Song
I used to have a friend

No one you'd care to meet
Sometimes we'd pretend
I could keep him off the street
I have a peaceful life ahead of me

Though we had funny ways
We knew each other's taste
We would fight for days
It filled up all the space
I have a peaceful life ahead of me

Now I have no more friend
We just ran out of luck
Would I do it again
Not for a million bucks
I have a peaceful life ahead of me

That year I met Antonia in November. On Christmas day, I helped moved her old boyfriend out (Lee Lamb. He invented the word "teenybopper" to commemorate the twelve-year-old runaways, who first hit the Village in the summer of '62. Hey Lee, where are you?). After helping him move, we all went to a Marx Brothers movie. He didn't know I was moving in after the movie. I thought if he knew I was interested, he might not consider leaving.

In early 1963, Antonia and I moved to 309 Houston Street in the Lower East Side, four rooms on the ground floor for $60 a month. It was right around the corner from the first place I lived on Clinton Street, when I came to New York in '59. That was $46 for four rooms on the fourth floor. We had been there for about two months before Weber showed up in May.

Antonia's plan was for us to play together on an ongoing basis, without making the overt suggestion that we do so. She didn't think it suitable for women to dictate regarding her man's work/gig, but she was fine about setting it up so we'd think it was our idea. She had no problem with being sneaky, which she felt was appropriate feminine behavior. Not for nothing one of her few relatives who (somewhat) understood her used to call her "sly boots". She finally explained to me that her partial motivation in introducing us was to keep Weber off the streets. Another factor was that she felt we had a lot to teach each other. She sure had that right.

Stories about Antonia. What about when she entered the Junior Scholastic poetry contest, and submitted a poem about mankind's next evolutionary step. Her poem won, but they refused to give the award, because "she couldn't possibly have really written it." She told them she did, they told her she was lying. So she sent her poem to science fiction writer Robert Heinlein, who sent her a reply congratulating her on a job well done.

But one of my favorite Antonia stories is the one about her destroying a dentist's office. This one goes back to a dentist in her family who enjoyed hurting people, especially children. He offered free dental service to all the kiddies in all the families. This is back in the days before lydocaine (trade name xylocaine), and high-speed water-cooled drills. You people who never experienced dental work in the forties and fifties have no idea how much it used to hurt, even if the dentist was trying not to. But this guy was really trying to. Needless to say, Antonia became phobic about dentists, and avoided them for years. Finally at the age of twenty, she was in dire need of dental work, and went to a new dentist, to whom she explained her problem. The dentist

43

suggested that she come on a Saturday with her husband (that marriage didn't last long), when he had no other clients, and get drunk first.

Antonia wasn't a drinker, but she liked Cointreau, an orange liquor. She sat in the dentist's chair and had several slugs from the bottle, but felt nothing. The dentist suggested more. Still nothing. By the time the bottle was half empty (on an empty stomach), she still felt nothing. So she finished the bottle. Then for the first and only time in her life, everything went black.

She woke up the next day to discover that she had attacked the dentist and completely destroyed the dentist's drill and office. She also kicked out his window. It took six cops and her husband to finally subdue her.

Her principle regret about all this was that it happened during a blackout, and she doesn't remember any of it.

Before I met Antonia, one of her boyfriends was a pot dealer named Hungarian Tom, who fled the abortive Hungarian revolution in the 50s after throwing Molotov cocktails at Russian tanks. His people used to smuggle pot across the Mexican border in a TV repair truck. Antonia's dad was a T-man, and used to talk to her about his work. He mentioned an upcoming bust of a TV repair truck at the Mexican border that he was working on, and she told Tom, who made sure that this time the truck was full of TV repair equipment. Big surprise for the Feds. Antonia's dad was enraged. Who could have possibly told them?

Sly Boots strikes again.

Antonia, the legend

Kathryn Frederick *(interview conducted July, 2003)*

I think tomorrow turns
With his toe
And you will shine and shine
Unspent and underground
        Diane Deprimna

Antonia's building was in a beautiful New York neighborhood that reflects prosperity and success. If only that were the case. Antonia is the talented unsung song master who saw the need to introduce two of the '60's craziest musicians to each other to form a whole.

Antonia opens the door wearing a blue denim dress and a bright yellow hat and invites us into her home that she shares with her five birds, two Quakers and three Cockatiels. She is surrounded with the things she loves, bookshelves floor to ceiling, full of vinyl and books. Her love of birds is evident even without the caged creatures from the many pictures throughout her apartment.

It is time for the birds to retire for the night. Antonia lovingly covers the cages that are almost as big as she and whispers a 'goodnight' to her children.

We go into the adjoining room so the birds may sleep. It's her bedroom. There are more books, a TV. Next to the television are videos of 'The Grapes of Wrath' and 'Black Stallion'. The magazines on her night stand show that her tastes haven't changed from her youth...*Bust* and *Cosmo* are on top. Her hat collection is on the dresser, colorful and fun.

We sit and get comfortable to start the interview.

Q: When did you start writing?

A: I always wrote, started as a child... before I could write I printed, before grade school. I wrote serials, essays, and songs. I would get up in front of the class and wing it. Everyone else would be prepared, but I would just wing it and make up my stories as I went. This gained me some leverage with the kids. They liked my stories.

Q: When were you first published?

A: Junior Scholastic, I received a statue. Once I won a poetry contest and was given a prize that was taken back because they decided the poem was too good and I couldn't possibly have written it. I was asked, "Did your father help you with this little girl?" I didn't show my parents anything I wrote. They wanted me to study scholastic things.

Q: Who was your father?

A: Sidney Goldblatt. He was an inspector for the Treasury. He was good. Not bribable. Very handsome. There was always a steady stream of young girls, my friends, coming to the house to see him. It annoyed me. He had charisma.

I sent a poem to Robert Heinlein. He was one of my heroes. He wrote me back, too, and thanked me for letting him read my poem.

I went to acting school for my own pleasure. I never wanted to be an actress. I would eat peyote and peanut butter sandwiches before I would go to class. I did that because Ronnie Chopman did. We'd meet in Central Park.

Q: How do you create your songs?

A: From fantasy, a mind picture. That's where 'Fucking Sailors in Chinatown' came from. A fantasy I had, also from the rhythm of words put together.

Q: Who have you collaborated with writing songs?

A: Steve Weber, Mark Johnson, hundreds of songs with Mark. Peter Stampfel, Gregory Alpert, a hot shit jazz sax player. Mark Johnson used to take about 88% of my lines out, saying they didn't work. Then one time while he was in the shower I was poking around and I found his song books and I saw that he put my lines back in and never told me. I didn't like that. I believe that credit should be given where credit is due.

Q: I've heard you worked with Bob Dylan.

A: No, not worked, but I used to have coffee with him and we shared ideas. We had a pure writing connection. Dylan wasn't a communicator unless he was writing music or singing. Communication wasn't something that came easily for him back then. I think he has gotten better with it over the years.

Q: How did you meet Steve Weber?

A: I had heard about the legendary Steve Weber and his groupies, male groupies who wanted to watch and hear him play 'Cocaine Blues' in double time. Steve was always barefoot and his guitar playing was amazing. He uses to be in Washington Park just walking around playing for the groupies. We met and went together off and on for two and a half years.

Q: How did you meet Peter Stampfel?

A: I was living with Lee Lamb and he introduced me to Peter, his best friend. Peter started courting me right away. He helped Lee move out and he and Lee went to a Marx Brothers movie. When the movie was over Peter moved in. We lived on 56th Street. Lee Lamb moved to the West Coast to be an astrologer.

Q: Did you and Peter write together?

A: Oh yes, Peter had it in his head that anything written after 1941 wasn't worth playing. I taught him, showed him that any music could be played if done with abandon, and to play on a banjo. He later decided he needed to add the fiddle and he just picked it up and played. I don't play an instrument so I had to tell Peter how the melodies should go. I couldn't show him.

Q: Did you introduce Steve and Peter to each other?

A: Yes. I knew Peter was missing a piece of himself and so was Steve, so I brought them together. They played a bit then went into the bedroom and didn't come out until they had written 'Bound to Lose.' Peter said to me after that, 'I feel I've found my brother'.

Q: I've heard you were a psychedelics guide?

A: Yes, it came with the territory, not necessarily a good guide. I never lost a patient.

Q: When did you meet Karen Dalton?

A: Midway. We saw each as two things, interconnected, because when I would bring a song around and she would sing it I wouldn't even recognize it. Karen said 'I'm the greatest living practitioner of your work.' She even taught me to sing a little, I can't sing you know, but she taught me a bit. She would take my songs hot off the griddle. She took 'Going to See the King' (a happy song about dying) around to churches. When she died something beautiful left the world and will never come back again.

I met Al Grossman during the New York blackout. We were having drinks, (sidecars) before the blackout and I went to the ladies room. The blackout came and Al came into the ladies room. We couldn't get out. He asked me if I was a witch.

Q: Antonia, what is your favorite song that you wrote?

A: 'Fucking Sailors in Chinatown', and I really like, 'Griselda'.

Q: Do you think Steve and Peter should have stayed with The Fugs?

A: No. I think it was good that they stepped out when they did.

Q: What songs do you hate to hear sung?

A: 'Antonette'. Every one thinks it's about me and it's not.

Q: What was written for you?

A: 'Halfa Mind'. Steve wrote that for me.

Q: Who are your heroes?

A: Tuli Kupferberg. He's a beautiful person, a wonderful poet, an individual. Bruce Springsteen, Joni Mitchell, I really like her songs, arrangements and her singing. Bob Dylan, country spirit.

Collaborating with Antonia

Mark Johnson

Multi-talented musician, vocalist, producer/arranger and filmmaker Mark Johnson was Antonia's primary songwriting "partner in crime" (her words) in the late 70's and early 80's.

Over the years Antonia has meant a great deal to all of us who know her and especially those of us who, like myself, have worked with her.

Antonia and I have written over fifty songs together. Not only that, but our song-writing sessions would last for ten hours sometimes. She'd come around to my home studio around seven or seven thirty in the evening, and we'd start writing a song. First we would talk about the characters in the song and what they were like, who they were and what their goals were. After a talking session first, we would have enough background to refer to when the actual lyrics and melody were brought up for consideration.

We were very well suited together, like-minded. We both knew and appreciated the doo-wop/acapella group style of music and would always wind up going there when we wrote together. Not just in music style but in tone and mood throughout. Of course we both brought other influences to the table as well, such as Antonia's love of cowboy songs or rhythm and blues. All in all it was a fantastic adventure for me, those all night sessions. Once we got a song written, I would go about making a recording of it as Antonia hung out and cheered me on.

Antonia was a vital part of those sessions, as she was at my shows in New York. If she could get to a show of mine, which she almost always did, she would send me a card and tell me about it afterward. I looked forward to those reviews because they were always so bright with promise and great encouragement. I owe her so much: I can never thank her enough just for that.

I learned a great deal from working with Antonia, to say the very least. She was so dead spot on when it came to getting the right line for a verse or chorus. Let me give you some examples of her work that only I know. We wrote many songs about relationships and the meaning of love and romance. One that comes to mind is a song called "Heartline:"

I'm calling on my Heart Line
In the hopes of reaching you tonight
Over miles and trials of dream time
And still I haven't got it right

You see, Antonia was a big fan of Peter Weir's film, *The Last Wave,* which deals with the aboriginal belief that dreams and waking time are equally real and important realms. Antonia was a true mystic in the pure sense of the word. At our best together, she gave language to my own mystical sense and I hope I was able to keep her interest as well. I will give you a list from memory of the song titles I can recall. There were many that were written and never made into a demo. I am sorry for that. Nothing lost really, because our time writing together was an educational affair. A study of ancient street corner values and desires, set to new melodies and stories. Antonia is my favorite collaborator, hands down. She reached out to me and took me up with her and allowed me to shape her ideas with mine. Working with Antonia is truly an experience I will never forget.

Bumping Into Peter and Antonia

Joshua Raoul Brody

In 1971 I was a bike messenger in New York City and ran into Peter – literally – on the sidewalk outside the apartment he and Antonia shared on West 55th Street. I recognized him because the previous summer I'd heard "Once a Year" on one of the freeform FM stations, took a liking to it, tracked down "Good Taste is Timeless," and then hied myself down to Folk City to catch the band.

Peter was unshaken by the bicycle bump but stirred by my recognition, and invited me up to meet the old lady. As I recall, Antonia was still in bed but was absolutely as gracious and unselfconscious as could be. The two of them plied me with tea, keenly noted my groupiedom, and fed it with anecdotes of the great, near-great, and far-great with whom they'd consorted, and extolled the virtues of perfume for men. As I was leaving they invited me to a jam in a Brooklyn garage that weekend, and Antonia pressed on me a shirt that Peter no longer wore. It was a long-sleeve pullover with broad tan and pink horizontal stripes.

The jam that weekend included Karen Dalton, started at 11 pm (ooh! late-night jam session with genuine hipsters!) and was interrupted periodically by some of the participants shooting speed (ooh! *drug-addled* hipsters!). Antonia and Peter showed me "I Disremember Quite Well" which Antonia sang in that haunting voice, and I remember the chords to this day.

Chapter Three: Letters

Notes, cards and letters sent to friends, sometimes at the pace of several per week, were so thoroughly woven into the fabric of Antonia's life that they constituted a sort of "blog" decades before the internet. Occasionally she would send a song or story, but more often it would be a vignette that captured an event or mood. Like all of us, sometimes she needed to vent, and would take pen to paper to do so. Many of her notes have the quality of a Zen koan, including a killer punch-line, which is why they were hard to throw away. We kept perhaps a quarter of the hundreds of notes we received from her in the course of 35 years. Other friends were gracious enough to share some of the letters they saved as well. What follows is a mix of letters and excerpts, in less than perfect order of chronology.

Until I read through Antonia's letters in one sitting, I never noticed how often she made reference to using speed. I asked her if she wanted these references left out, but she characteristically rejected censorship in any form.

I'm sick. I've got a chest & nose cold, & I feel pretty down. But I'm better today than I was yesterday, so I guess I'll survive.

On Wed, the coldest May Day in history, the band played an outdoor street festival. It rained, too, but a good time was had by all. I was too sick to attend.

On Thurs, the band played at Max's Kansas City, a hip bar with $2.75 hamburgers & drink prices to match. Almost the only people who came were our friends – ½ the audience was old friends, no kidding. The band had to pay full price for drinks. I wanted to go to this gig a lot, so I took a bunch of speed & went. I was glad to see my friends, but by the end of the first set I was so woozy that I had to go home. That night I reveled the worst of my sickness out – speed is good for infectious diseases.

There are many "might have beens" in the letters – films that were never made, albums that were not recorded.

---

2 weeks ago I couldn't spell filmmaker and now I are one!

Met a lady photographer named Trixie who was doing a 15 minute film about a teen-age girl. She was having trouble writing the script since she is primarily into visuals. I reworked the script, added 2 songs, and her film became our film. Trixie is primarily gay & lives with her girlfriend, Peggy, a musician. It is really strange to go there for a "hen party," because they talk about women they have loved, & I am such a lover of men – I've never even made love to a woman. But with patience & humor, we get along.

… That ain't all. Our manager Stig is writing a slick, full-length humorous porno film, & Peter & I will help with the writing. It will probably be called "Have Moicy" & the band will provide the background music. So far Stig has accepted 7 of our ideas & 4 songs...

Just finished an incredible 6 day music blast, going house to house of my music friends, exchanging songs, playing records, getting high, and talking about making records. Coco called it the Idiot Wind Music Festival. Hunt and I wrote a song that I want on the record called "Lookin'." All my friends want to play on my record and it just can't be done...

The drought ended Fri night & I celebrated by writing a song with Chris Anderson (Black Blind Crippled Chris). He's a jazz piano player & writes beautiful music in Old Standard ballad style.

Rounder is interested in an Antonia record but I just got the word that they will not work with Karen in any way, shape or form. Just because she got high & pulled the bathroom sink out of the wall before she passed out last time

56

(TRUTH). Well, she's the best gal singer I know, <u>and</u> my oldest friend, & I guess I am going to have to jeopardize my record and insist on her…

Here is the note that gave birth to the title of this collection of writings.

LATE SAT. NITE

I'm doing my homework – John S, Peter's new guitar player, wants to write a song combining a talking blues & a rap song. I haven't heard much rap music (except Blondie) so I am listening to a soul station to hear some. None have played yet, but right now there's a song whose entire lyric is "don't stop (grunt) don't stop (grunt)."

John S is working on music for "Showoff" (my lyric) and hopes to entice Joyce the Voice to learn it. (note: John S and Joyce the Voice – rather new characters in this farce/drama. I said I wanted to write a book of barely-connected stories, essays, etc. called BEAR SUIT FOLLIES. Well, I don't think it's a book after all, I think it's my life, so I will try to introduce new characters, plot lines & stuff accordingly)…

I'm suffering from a bad case of the GIMME'S – rabid lust for material possessions. 2 good words about STUFF – I'm inheriting a functioning vacuum cleaner from my dead uncle, & Peter & Betsy are lending me a TV set that works…

Frustrations with Jimmy gave birth to many a note...

AAARRGGH! My friend Jimmy (A/K/A Vaporhead) has been staying on my couch. This morning he fell asleep during his morning cigarette and set my bloody couch on FIRE! BRAGGH! He's lucky I have lots of practice holding my temper. He's out right now pricing mattresses or maybe he's running for his life. As if that wasn't enuf, we have no hot water today. I'm making spaghetti sauce, & when I poured the grease off in the sink it coagulated & turned white and stayed there! GAAH!

Wowie Zowie

My old friend & house guest Jimmy (A/K/A Vaporhead) has cigarette-burned his way through 2 mattresses & dropped cherry pits all over the floor where I can step on them with my bear feet. He has promised to do about 90 things for me, & has actually done about 2 ½. I haven't had so much lip service since Peter left. He's full of good intentions, but so is the road to hell. The phone rings all day & all night for Jimmy, but he will pay my phone bill, he says...

MIDNIGHT SUNDAY

Pad Pad Pad CHING WOOSH! SLOPSLOPSLOPSLOP –

"Who dat?"

That's Speed Queen, the midnight marauder of the basement laundry room. *Her* dirty laundry won't stand the light of day. She threw out 2 burnt bedsheets tonight – blames it on her friend Jimmy. Bet you could roll up them bedsheets and smoke 'em. Har har...

Howdy, here I am coming out from behind my character. And Jimmy did fall asleep while smoking TWICE & burned through 2 mattresses... But tonight I visited Karen for a short time & she sang "The Sun Ain't Gonna Shine Anymore" and made the universe perfect for awhile.

58

When Antonia was 16, she gave birth to a daughter who was immediately put up for adoption. Many years later that daughter tracked her down and asked to meet. After meeting they maintained sporadic contact for several years.

LATE FRI

Well, we have a date. I'm going to meet my daughter on Wed. the 6th at the adoption agency. I'm trying not to expect anything in particular, because whatever I expect, the reality is bound to be different...I got a beautiful thick warm fake snow leopard coat that is big enough in the shoulders and biceps. HOORAY. Gave my outgrown but nifty other coat to new neighbor Sharon, who is big but not as big as the Bear. I have gall stones... Can't win 'em all.

WED

I just met my daughter & her husband. Her name is Ronni (not a nickname), his is Steve. We met at the adoption agency. She is painfully thin – 114 lbs – but says this is fat for her, she usually weighs 90-94. She has considerable insight into herself on an intellectual level, probably gained recently, between the shrink and the lithium...

Antonia faced increasingly challenging health problems as the years passed, ultimately resulting in her relocation to Florida, where she presently resides in an assisted-living facility. She worked hard at maintaining a positive, hopeful spirit through all her medical ups and downs (mostly downs), but at times her fortitude was sorely challenged.

I am in very bad shape. Got spasm all though my body, can't go outside. Peter is out of town for 10 days. A neighbor is doing the shopping for me. All I can do is hang out in bed and listen to the radio. The doctors don't know what it is yet. Also, I'm straight (no drugs)…

This will be short, because it is hard to write. 2 days ago I had 3 teeth pulled on sodium pentothal. But yesterday I took a codeine pill for the pain & was sick as a dog for 12 hours. Peter is cutting a record with the old Rounders. It is going well. I am going to have my head shrunk. Dr. Summers specializes in treating creative artists. Should be interesting. Still have the spasms. Can't sit up or get around much – I just hang out in bed. It is very boring, especially since Peter is gone all day & night cutting the album.

Things are looking up. I'm on a physical improvement & Get My Shit Together kick. On Tues, I will have my last 5 teeth removed. GOOD RIDDANCE to bad rubbish…

Finally figured out how to eat cashew nuts without teeth. Roll 'em up in a paper towel & take a hammer & WHOMP 'em. Pulverizes 'em & releases your aggression all at once…

My folks are in town. They brought their car to shuttle me around to doctors. Got a 2 ½ hour neurological checkup yesterday. They confirmed the opinion of my own doctor – it's a side effect of taking Stelazine, with no known treatment. So they are trying different drugs on me, hoping to find a combination that works. Roll on, River of Shit! Peter, Betsy, and I are cooking turkey dinner for my folks on Thanksgiving. None of us ever made turkey before. Wish us luck…

Monday Morning at the Gastro-Intestinal Clinic

Up to the Bronx in the early morning rain. My chart (medical records) has disappeared. My doctor wasn't in. Went to the nurse, the nurse said a curse, and that's the end of Rin Tin Tin...

In the Fall of '76 various medical problems and an upcoming concert by Bruce Springsteen and the E Street Band were on a sad collision course.

AARGH! Bruce S. Concert N.Y. SOLD OUT before I even heard about it! I have all my friends searching for tickets, because if I don't see something clean soon I will *die*. All the men in NY are wimps or pansies or both. Also I am physically unable to sit through a concert. So if I have a ticket I will *have to* get better by the end of Oct...

I got tickets for the Springsteen concert Oct. 28! I went to a scalper and paid an *astronomical* sum for them. 4 of us are going. I am not in shape to sit through a concert – but I intend to be in shape by the 28th. Wish me luck.

I had a growth cut out of the top of my mouth. It was too big to take out all at once, so I go back next Weds to have the rest of it removed. PFUI. The only people I see these days are doctors and dentists.

I was unable to go outside for 5 days, but this morning I was improved & took a walk to 57th St. Wow! It was like getting out of prison. Peter has been incredibly helpful.

I had 3 skin cancers removed 3 days ago. It was done under a local anesthetic so I didn't have to stay overnight in the hospital. It was scary as hell. They cut out such a big slice of me that they had to plot for an hour in order to figure out how to sew me up! Tomorrow I go back to have the bandage changed & the drains removed. I am in pain but I figure it will be better tomorrow. The spasms are easing up a little. HOORAY. It looks like I may be able to go to the Springsteen concert for real!

I went into the clinic to have my chest checked. I had several skin cancers removed from my chest & right boob. Anyway, the wound was infected & they put me right in the hospital. Thurs. night was the Springsteen concert & I MISSED IT. 4 of us were going to go to the concert & I was going to make a loin of pork dinner beforehand. Peter made the pork and it came out great – he brought me a piece yesterday. Peter and my friends brought me a big poster of Bruce which now decorates my hospital wall. I will probably be in here a couple of weeks…

Certainly one of the most significant changes in Antonia's life came when Peter ended their romantic relationship and married Betsy, with an awkward period of transition in-between. Since these letters are not in chronological order, there are many jumps among "before," "after" and "in-between." This note was written on the final day of 1976.

New Year's Eve

It's the usual mad scene. The Unholies are going to play Franconia NH this New Year's weekend. They still have no vehicle. Bill (manager) was going to drive them, but his wife hurt her back & he couldn't leave her stranded in the country with 2 little kids. Thank God, the club called this AM & rented a van for our guys. The van was late, of course. Hope they make it to NH by midnight.

I'm spending New Year's Eve at Betsy's (best friend) in the Village. It's 18 degrees today, going to 10 tonight, so I probably won't get around much. But it beats being alone. I am getting around a little better these days. Improvement! The band wants to change its name. When the old Rounders were in town they rapidly gained such a bad rep. that many clubs won't hire the Unholies due to the similar name. Betsy suggested "The Riot Act," which I like. I suggested "Peter & the Lost Boys" from Peter Pan.

January, 1977

Hi Ho – what a magical night. Tues. nights are usually bummers, because Peter plays at B'way Charlie's and I can't go. So this Tuesday I decided to see the movie "Rocky" with Betsy instead of sitting home feeling sorry for myself. What a good idea! What a good movie! ...a story with heart: I'm a sucker for "heart."

Back at my apt., Betsy's getting ready to go home, we hear a scratching at the door. We open it, & a strange adorable little animal comes in. Turns out to be an African ferret, owned by somebody I've been wanting to meet – new neighbor Dennis on the 2nd floor. Dennis is a percussionist – rhythm guitarist – songwriter – session man. 24 years old, café au lait color, small, lively and Scooter all the way. We promise to exchange songs. Now if I can only figure out why the ferret climbed up 5 flights of stairs to scratch at my front door?

July, 1977.

Thursday night was the final performance of the Rounders. It was at the Bottom Line & all our friends came. Betsy and I bought a cake to wish everyone good luck. The band played very well, and it was real nice. Looks like we are really going to Wisconsin at the end of this month. Peter and Betsy will start driving on the 27th & I'll fly and meet them in Milwaukee on the 30th.

Betsy, forgive me for including this one!

…What a silly night I had last night. Betsy and I went to the Super Fly Boutique, a clothing store on charming 42nd Street that caters to pimps. We both got metallic iridescent emerald green jackets. They were on sale. We got Peter a blue-green shirt with orange bomber planes & a big purple bomb on it. Then we went to a sporting goods store where Betsy bought a bust developer & I got a screaming yellow hat, the kind hunters wear to avoid getting shot. Then we bought some porno books, went home & ate Brussels sprouts & English muffin pizzas, & dyed my hair impossibly red. Wow! Hope you're happy too.

Two years later. Tanith Lee is a fantasy author whose work was then published by Betsy's firm.

Tanith Lee is staying at Peter and Betsy's. They are throwing a party for her tonight. Think I will be nasty and go to it…

Both before and after Peter moved out an interesting cast of characters passed through Apartment 7P.

Girl fan of Peter's came to visit last night. A "professional musician's friend," used to be a dominatrix (professional mistreater of men). Real name Joanie, professional name Satana. Once she had a 40-year old "john" who wanted to be humiliated. She put a collar on his neck & ordered him to get down on all fours like an animal. He began to bark like a dog, hoping to please her. She said, "Any fool can bark. Meow like a cat." He began to meow, and she berated him because he didn't sound like a real cat. He tried for 45 minutes, & finally produced a good feline-sounding wail. Satana then kicked him in the ass as hard as she could and screamed, "I *hate* cats!"

Although Antonia never had much money, she loved to shop (as her trip to the Super Fly Boutique with Betsy attests). She still does.

I finally have enough clothes to make it through the rest of the winter in style (?) Got a chalk-pink Ban-lon sweater from Peter for Valentine's Day. I got him a badly-needed Pendleton type wool shirt. I gave it to him early, and he's worn it every day since, in bed, in the bath tub, he never takes it off...

What a blessing! My Mom came up to stay with me for a week, cause Peter's mixing the new album all day and playing at Folk City all night. I still can't use trains or buses, & taxis are expensive. But Mom and I took a taxi to Macy's and I had a small but nifty spending spree. I got a pair of red & white checked panties, perfect for playing Farmer's Daughter, and a pair of shell-pink panties with beige lace trim, suitable for a French whore...

I got my Spring wardrobe – a pair of Kelly green slacks, a green tank top with white daisies on it, & a pink t-shirt with a full color picture of Bruce Springsteen. And my motorcycle jacket. Wow!

Fashion note – I got blue bell-bottom slacks with white stars on them, & a black t-shirt with ROCK & ROLL in big silver letters across the boobs.

Bear With You (Professional Collaboration Service *ON APPROVAL*)

ZIPLESS FINISHING

Many people have a flash of inspiration and begin a song with one or two great verses and perhaps even a bridge and then go dry and can't get a finish. We will provide GUARENTEED a first-rate finish so much in your style that even your BEST FRIENDS won't know where you put it down and we picked it up. We can make endings to demonstrate, imply, or provide any philosophical, religious, or political theory or hypothesis, based on the work you did at the beginning of the song. "Deeper meaning" last verses to complete "ordinary level" beginnings. "Surprise" endings – the content of your beginning turned inside out. MORAL SERVICE – *any* moral principal demonstrated in "CUTESY" kid's style or "DRY WRY" adult fashion. "BLUE DINOSAUR" endings – guaranteed to have 100% pure NOTHING to do with anything else in the song – confound the critics! Extraneous, dense, or stupid plot material removed. Obtuse verse clarified.

SPECIALTIES – Pep up your boring trite lyrics with a striking image or flash of insight when they least expect it! Pass yourself off as a Writer with Promise!

This was sent to Maggie Roche. Antonia sometimes made multiple copies of letters that contained carefully-crafted stories and sent them to several people.

Legend of the Good-Time Bears (a true story)

One day when I was walking through the Village, I passed a promising-looking Gift Shoppe. My eye was caught by a mug, oatmeal-colored with brown bears on it. As I looked closer, I realized that the bears were having an orgy! I *had* to have it, but I had no money, so I just kept walking. But I came back once a week for four weeks, just to make sure it was there. On the fifth week, I had the money, and I rushed downtown to claim my prize. I looked in the window, and OMIGAWD! It was gone! I went inside and was greeted by a very nelly salesman. I asked about the mug with the bears having an orgy on it. "You must be in the wrong store," he said. "We don't have any such item."

"Well, I know you did," I said. "It was in your window for four weeks."

"I'll ask the Boss," he said. The Boss was magnificent. Tall and portly, with his silver-white hair combed into an elaborate pompadour, he moved through the store like an ocean liner. I inquired about the bear orgy mug, and he winced. "I believe we have that item in the stockroom," he said, "But I wish you wouldn't say that the bears are having an orgy, We don't want to –"

I cut him off. "Well, what do *you* think those bears are doing?"

He stopped a minute, then said, "I prefer to think – they are just – having a good time."

So there you have it.

In this letter to Maggie, Antonia captured one of those small moments filled with wonder.

Its Halloween night, and the last few drag queens are staggering home in their finery. The streets were manic and mobbed all day. I went to the Zoo in the afternoon, in the spring-like 65 degree sunshine. The atmosphere changed suddenly & we had a beautiful clear windy autumn night. Walking through the mob on 8th Ave, I saw an apparition coming toward me – a man & a woman walking with a huge black chow. Heads turned to look at the dog – in the twilight he seemed to be a mythical beast, or a remnant of some braver time. He was so black he seemed to absorb the light around him. Head up, tail up, he walked into the wind, & my heart stopped for a beat. Then he passed, and his world passed with him, and I went down to the "A" train & headed for the Village.

Speaking of zoo visits, Antonia, A/K/A "Singing Bear," loves bears of all types. Here is one of Bear's bear stories, again courtesy of Maggie:

Cub of a Different Color

As you can see, I am a brown bear. I live in a bar-free "cage" with Duchess and Big Brown. A deep dry moat separates us from the humans. Another one separates us from the white bears.

As far as racism goes, we bears follow the "equal but separate" policy. We mate with our own kind. But I have always been attracted to white boys, with their tiny ears & long, snakelike necks. Especially Nanook, who lives in the next enclosure. So, when I came into heat, I jumped into the moat. By bracing my back against the wall, I was able to climb up into Nanook's pen. We really raised some hell until the keeper caught us.

When little Snoot was born, Duchess really gave me the fish-eye. "That cub is mighty pale for a Kodiak bear," she sniffed. I put the claws to her nose. She won't be doing any sniffing for a while.

And what of little Snoot? I'm banking on a new world for her, a future where all bears will run free.

Antonia has focused on various people as primary correspondents through the years. Since 2002, her friend Corona, now residing in Eugene, Oregon, has been one of the people Antonia has communicated with most frequently. Now a custom milliner, Corona performed in clubs in and around Portland for a number of years, hearing many stories about Antonia. They struck up a correspondence, exchanged tapes and songs, and became close friends. This sequence of letters traces Antonia's transition from NYC to Sarasota, Florida.

(from New York)

2002

It's a nice day. I'm lying here watching the secrets of the elephants' migration. I got a Chinese jacket – fuchsia with gold embroidery… I signed up for a class in writing erotica and pornography. As you probably know, I have written this stuff in the past. I want to do it again, but it would take dynamite down there to get me moving again…

The "erotica class." Standing room only. The speaker was a sexual outlaw (like me). Her talk was basically about how to find a market for our stuff. The stuffed vulva. I saw one this summer. It was beautiful, and yes, it was a work of art…

2003

(the interview Kathryn conducted during this visit is included elsewhere in this collection)

It's hot and sweaty here, & even the birds take a long nap in the afternoon. I had a visit from Sandra Koppell, Kathryn Frederick & Norman. We talked about the birth of the Rounders. Next day, Barbara Beeman's Band was playing at the Bistro & I went. I wore my Best Hat & got lots of compliments…

The folk fest sounds great. Its *centuries* since I've done anything like that. I'm re-reading my Arabian horse magazines. I have full-time home attendants, both from Jamaica. May Lin is sturdy, great in a crisis, a good cook, watches TV with me, & can be a lot of fun (as long as I "behave"). She's reading "Sister Souljah." Maury, who does weekends, is a more down person, does not watch TV, & is reading "God Will Make A Way." I get to go out for a walk every day (supervised). One problem – these ladies arrive at 9:00 AM every day. I am still in "bear mode" at that time & am about as personable as any bear whose sleep has been interrupted. I make a mighty effort to behave with human decency – these ladies do not need to be greeted by a bear...

(How odd to find ourselves mentioned in this letter! The picture of Antonia in her "Best Hat," designed and made by Corona, appears in the photo section.)

Your letter sounds like you're in the middle of a lot of fun too. I loved the hat pictures too. This is the day after the blackout. Thank God I was home when it happened. John & Susan from Wisconsin (& the Rounders list) were supposed to visit – haven't seen them in 14 years. Buses & trains were out, but they were on E. 40th St & they walked the rest of the way here! We ate my (melting) boysenberry sorbet as the sun went down. I lit a big bear candle from years ago. My friends took pictures in the dark. I was wearing my Best Hat...

We've got flying chaos here. I'm getting ready to move to Sarasota, Fla. Tommy Tune, the foundling cockatiel, is going with me. I'm pulling up roots, I've lived here for 35 years! I'm leaving 95% of my stuff behind. I'm leaving all my WINTER STUFF!

(from Antonia's Sarasota apartment)

I apologize for taking so long to answer you. Hurricane Charley was close, but not a direct hit. Neighbors came out the next day asking, "Is this your first hurricane?" Today we just missed Hurricane Frances. I get it – these are tropical storms & I am living in a tropical climate! A fantasy come true...

This letter is a celebration. I bought a baby Quaker that is bright pink, covered with pin feathers, & topped with a big beak. She was the only hen in this group, & she walked over her brothers & fought with them. I love the outrageous little Quaker hens, nothing stops them…

While Antonia loved the Sarasota climate (NYC winters had become increasingly hard for her), she struggled with the challenges of independent living, particularly with taking her medications, nutrition, and hydration. She suffered a major collapse, and after a prolonged hospitalization her cousin (and legal guardian) Geri arranged a long-term stay in a nursing home, where Antonia slowly regained her strength.

(from the nursing home)

It's weird here. I'm glad that I can talk to you about it. I'm in the hospital (?) Rest home (?) It's been a very busy place since I arrived. But 2 days ago the sun went down & it didn't come up. It's black as the ace of spades out there. And the hospital is deserted. Your hat found a good home. My roommate is a woman named Kay, who was a fashion editor…

How you doing? I'm doing pretty well. They moved me from the east wing (psycho ward) to the west side (people who have been hurt but are still competent). I was in the wacky ward because they had no other place to put me, but it almost did me in. The nights were never "silent," but full of screams, begging, weeping, etc. It was almost enough to make a day-person out of me. The food here is pretty good, & you have a choice. Tomorrow I will visit Tommy Tune, who is being fostered by a cockatiel breeder.

71

Peter is coming down here for the Sarasota Film Festival in April, so I'll probably see him. I have to sign out (or in) when I go out (or in) but its all in good fun.

Love, d'bear

Antonia adjusted well to the nursing home, taking on the role of "pusher" for residents who were confined to wheelchairs. After careful consideration of all options (and an obscene amount of paperwork), Geri made arrangements for Antonia to reside in an assisted-living facility on a permanent basis.

(from Cabot Reserve)

This is my address and phone #. The place is big, with big grounds, but my apt. is as small as a kitty litter box. I put up a bird feeder near my window, but no bird has landed yet. The "human" food here could be better, but the strawberries are in season…

Antonia has adjusted to life in Cabot Reserve. She is able to take trips to favorite haunts – restaurants, shops, pet stores – most days, watches nature programs on television, reads, listens to music, and attempts to be patient, kind and helpful. She very much remains "Singing Bear," dancing to her own unique drummer. Drop her a note: you just might get one in return!

Chapter Four: Photographs

Antonia the drama student, circa 1960, just beginning to make her presence
felt in the Village.

Another picture from the same photo sesson.

In the Iris Gardens, Montclair, NJ, 1983.

A favorite picture from girlhood. There was a firehouse near her Brooklyn home.

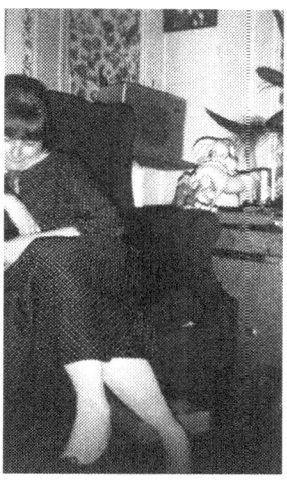

Surrounded by her Stuff, 1982.
"My favorite patchwork shirt!"

1982 in her apartment, looking winsome:
a favorite picture of Antonia's.

With her young friend Kodiak, 1991. A
fitting name for a friend of Singing Bear!

Antonia with Susan, Kate and Colin
McFadden at an Italian Street
Festival, 1986.

Antonia and our son, Colin, 1992: two Trekkies!

1999: "Me and my Dodger, my Dodger and me; we're just as happy as birds in a tree."

Antonia eye-to-eye with feathered friend, 2006.

Me with Antonia during the Great New York Blackout, August, 2003. She grabbed her Best Hat, made by friend Corona, just before the picture was taken: always stylish!

Antonia when I visited her in September, 2006.

The same day, with her "wig hat on her head". She wears
it only for special occasions.

Chapter Five: Stories, Poems, and Articles

Early Poetry

Until her creative energy began to focus on songs, Antonia wrote quite a bit of poetry, of which only a modest amount survives, including these examples. "Duji" is slang for heroin...

Changes – July 14, 1964

Leaves and sea winds meet in me –

I have absorbed myself whole

Time trickles down the back of my throat

(It tastes like cocaine).

Corner of the eye things have taken the center stage

And part of me is always flowing underground.

I tried everything. I went sane for awhile, but

it made the birds stop coming to my window, so I stopped.

I play elaborate games with time now.

I wear it looped through my ears

or pretend it lives in my wrist watch.

The calendar says summer,

But all my colors are rust brown.

They say it is the year of Television and Duji.

Changes – July 24, 1964

Sometimes
        late at night
I hear someone calling outside my window
  and sometimes it is you
    and sometimes me
and I sail the 20 stories to the ground.
The eyes of past cats mark my path
and I can move backward as well as forward
I run through night with night in my guts
  and sometimes I meet you
    and sometimes me
and often it doesn't matter which.

The **Bo Breslin Stories.** *There are several versions of the circumstances surrounding" the Bo Breslin stories," some written jointly by Peter and Antonia and some by Antonia alone. As good a version as any claims that the original plan was to write a novel, with chapters alternating between Bo's sexual and musical education, but only the "sex" ones got written because they were immediately salable in the new, tabloid porn publications like* **Screw** *and* **Kiss**. *Of the four Bo stories of which I am aware, three appear below. "Wicked Arabella" was included in the liner notes of the HMR album, "Alleged in their own Time" (incorrectly and infuriatingly shortened to "Arabella"). ""Topless Dancer" and "My first Interview" were published in* **Kiss** *and written by Antonia alone. Not included here is "Marybeth's Dreadful Ordeal," available by request to purchasers of the HMR album, "* **Last Round**.*" It was written by Peter and Antonia in an all-night tag team session fueled by pots of strong tea. It is three times longer than the other Bo stories, and far more, well, disturbing. That is, if you find the sexual abuse of twelve-year old girls disturbing. Bo completists may contact the editor for a copy.*

Wicked Arabella

By Peter Stampfel and Antonia

Arabella! What magic that name conjures up in my mind.   Images of rosy-tipped breasts and moonshine thighs float before my mind's eyes.

Arabella used to be my babysitter. By the time I was twelve, however, she was babysitting my sister Griselda. I was too manly to require such attentions. Still, I think it reassured my parents that "the sitter" was there.

When I was twelve, Arabella was seventeen, a fine, ripe piece of girlflesh. She was a high-school dropout, and worked as a cashier in the movie house during the day. Babysitting gave her a little extra income, and she was good with kids.

She had a wild reputation, and I'm sure she lived up to it. She excited my boyish fantasies by wearing a black bra under her white blouse. Dark stockings too, on strong, well-shaped legs. I can see it now.

My favorite time of night was bedtime, when she was around. Although she was officially my sister's sitter, she would give me a good-night kiss when it was time to go to bed. After I turned twelve, she began putting some tongue into those good-night kisses. She had a devilish nature.

At twelve, I was, sadly, a virgin. I was as unwilling a virgin as you'll ever meet, and I hinted to my friends about my hot exploits, but I was a virgin nonetheless.

One night, Arabella showed up without the black bra on. As I surreptitiously watched the jiggling of her large breasts, I realized that she wasn't wearing a bra at all. I glanced at my father to see if he had noticed, but his face was normal. Maybe he was getting old. Anyway, my parents left soon afterward.

We spent the evening with the TV blasting the kind of stuff that Griselda liked. She's a pretty good sister, but you know how 9 year old kids are. If you're 12, they get in your hair. I went to my room to practice my guitar.

Pretty soon there was a knock on the door of my room. It was Arabella. "Well, Bo," she said, "your sister's asleep. My chores are finished for the night. Will you join me in a coke?"

We went to the refrigerator. There was only one coke left. "Never mind, we'll share it," said Arabella. She took the first drink, licking the rim of the bottle with a wicked pink tongue. My eyes were glued to every move she made, and she was enjoying the sense of power.

"Will you get me a cigarette?" she asked. Would I! I would have gone to the ends of the earth for her. I got one for her and one for myself, and we sat smoking in slightly uncomfortable silence. I watched the shadow of her nipples through the blouse.

She turned to me suddenly. "Bo, have you ever had a woman?" She was smiling. "Yeah, a few," I lied.

"Do the girls like you?"

"Yeah." They did, too.

"I bet you've learned a lot." I didn't mind the mild sarcasm because she delivered the line with one of the most evil smiles I have ever seen. She was truly the dark princess of evil smiles.

"What was that record you were playing before?"

"Oh… Bo Diddley."

"Sure sounded wild."

Inspiration! "Want to hear it again?"

The phonograph was, of course, in my room. "Love to."

I let her walk first so I could wipe my sweaty palms on my jeans. Not only had I been fantasizing about her since I had a bald crotch, she was the star of the hottest wet dream I ever had. My mouth went dry and my feet seemed miles below my head.

We got to my room and I put the Bo Diddley on again. She sat down on the bed, leaning back voluptuously against the pillow. I could see most of the way up her skirt. There was a stack of records between me and Up Her Skirt. It was the stack of records I was learning guitar from. Chuck Berry, Elmore James, Muddy Waters, Howlin' Wolf, Mickey Baker. I played along and copped licks with my acoustic Gibson. My folks wouldn't let me have an electric because they were pissed at me for quitting the piano. I went through the albums like a rosary while sneaking peaks up her skirt, down her legs, up higher, down harder, God Damn! No fuckin' panties! Hotcha, I thought, crawling into bed.

"Why don't you put some of those records you were looking at on the phonograph? We can have a little concert."

I coolly fell out of bed and put on a Howling Wolf and a Muddy Waters. O so evil she smiles. Dark lady of my baddest dreams dissoloosely lying in my trundle bed. Trundle, trundle. Slow and cool I return to bed without falling on my face.

"Bo, honey," she whispered hoarsely, "could you make it a little darker?" In a trance of inspiration I went to the attic to fetch my Mickey Mouse night light. Off goes the ceiling, on glows Mickey trundle trundle back to bed.

"I spell M," says Bo Diddley, "…A…N…MAN…"

Arabella and me and Mickey and Bo Diddley. Yankee heaven of my lost cherry. Midwestern paradise of my adolescence. Sigh.

The goodnight kiss revisited. Son of goodnight kiss. More moist, more hot, yet deeper and paradoxically slippery yet sticky. She's got this low husky growl in her throat and she starts probing with her tongue like she's tryin' to split my head in two. I mean my head is so full of her tongue it's like to explode. Just in time she takes it out, leaving my mouth an easy ten degrees hotter. Her smile has changed from evil princess to evil queen. Real slow she unbuttons the top button of her blouse. And slower the second. The third bares her cleavage, the fourth and fifth glorify it. Her tits are firm as one could wish and her nipples jut upwards and a little away from each other. She pulls one out and offers it to me by pointing her nipple at my mouth and going, "mmmmmm?" low as a bee's buzz. I go at it like I'm inventing sucking from whole cloth. I'm trying to get her whole tit in my mouth and furthermore am convinced that I can. She thwarts my attempt with her other one. I nurse that awhile, then she pulls it out and puts my head in between them. I can't believe how good it smells in there. She takes off her blouse and my pajama top. Our bare chests get to be against each other for awhile. I'm fondling the place where top of stocking meets top of thigh, still a tactile favorite. Gathering courage to finger her honeypot. She got her hand on my ass & she squeezing it in this punishing-it-for-being-naughty way that should be too hard but somehow never is. Then she shoves her tongue in my head one more time and rips off my pajama bottoms with a single strong tug. I almost shit. I was embarrassed because of my terrific hard-on. I had some sort of notion that it wasn't cool. But Arabella sort of accidentally brushed against it with her hand, and then I knew she didn't mind. Her skirt had worked up to her thighs, and I was regretting the dim lighting. I had never had the chance to see a real live cunt before. I mean, I had peeked at my sister's, but she didn't even have hair yet.

"Why don't you get out of that hot old skirt," I suggested helpfully. "It's gonna get all wrinkled."

"Good thinking." She kissed me playfully on the nose and got out of bed. She turned her back to me. Slowly, slowly she slid the skirt down her round brown hips, over her thighs, past her knees, and off. A black garter belt and the dark stockings remained. Oboy. She picked up the skirt and turned to face me, holding the skirt in front of her like a stripper. She wiggled lasciviously behind the protective material. Then she threw the skirt across the room.

Cunt! The first clear view of Arabella's charming black bush shines brighter in my mind than a thousand divine revelations. I ran to her and embraced her madly, knocking us both to the floor. My prick must have a homing instinct of its own, because as we hit the floor I found myself tight inside her juicy box. Not one to quibble with fate, I began to pound away.

"Bo, what are you doing?" she protested. "Not on the floor!"

I wasn't hearing any of that shit. I may have been 12 years old, but I wasn't stupid. The Bo Diddley record had got stuck, playing "I'm a man" over and over. I started to laugh, then she started to laugh, and there we were, rollin' around on the floor and laughing and humping and pumping till, with a tremendous whoop, I shot my hot load right into her twisting little cunt.

I heard a gasp in the doorway. I looked up. There was my sister, Griselda. She was bug-eyed.

"What are you doing with your CLOTHES OFF?" she demanded.

"Wrestling," I replied with all the cool I could muster.

"Who won?" she wanted to know.

I stood up and gave her my nicest smile. "If you breathe a word of this to anybody, I'll mutilate you. Now get back to bed!"

Griselda knows my temper, especially when I smile. She left, fast.

All was in order by the time my parents got home. "Griselda was a perfect angel," Arabella told my mother on her way out.

"Bo was good too."

Topless Dancer

By Antonia
*(Originally published in **Kiss** Vol. 1 #24)*

It was my first night as a topless dancer. I was scared shitless.

I had never been naked in front of strangers before. Especially a crowd of strangers. I didn't feel ashamed, just tense. And I knew I would dance better if I was relaxed. I am proud of my body and thought I would enjoy showing it off, once I got used to it. And I love music. I wanted a job where I could be around live music all the time. And dancing seemed like more fun that cocktail waitressing. And topless paid better than regular dancing.

So there I was, hurrying to the Flight Club. I was early, but I wanted to be. I wanted a chance to warm up and get used to the club before the customers came in.

The Flight Club has a sort of psychedelic strobe-light décor. It was a minute before I could make out Ronnie, the club's owner, in the flashing light. "Where's the dressing room?" I asked him.

"Over there," he said, pointing vaguely to the left. I groped my way through the swirling lights to the door he had indicated and went in. A young man was in there, changing strings on a guitar.

"Where's the other dressing room?" I asked him. I was new to the café business.

"This is it," he announced. "These cheap dives never have more than one. Are you the dancer?"

"Yes. How did you know?"

He glanced at my large breasts, then looked away. "I just guessed. You have natural rhythm." He paused a moment. "Well, I'm Bo Breslin. My band's playing here tonight."

"I know. I came to see you two days ago. My name's Willie Mae."

"Have you danced in a lot of places around here?" "No. To tell you the truth, this is my first dancing job."

He grinned at me. "Are you scared?"

I decided to be honest. He seemed so friendly. "Yes, I'm nervous as hell. I never had any kind of nude job before."

"Never did any nude modeling or anything?"

"No."

"Then what did you do it for?" He seemed really curious.

"Well, I wanted a job where I could hear live music. And I can dance real good."

"Good reasons. Don't feel bad about it. It's just showing off, and showing off is fun."

"I feel a little embarrassed about liking to show off so much."

"Why? Showing off is good for you. Gets rid of those nasty ole inhibitions. I do it all the time myself. Every time I go on stage. I even play guitar in front of a mirror sometimes."

I laughed. I felt much more relaxed. "But now," I asked him, "will you get out of the dressing room so I can get into my G-string?"

"Gotta get these guitar strings changed. And the strobe lights out there make me seasick. But I'll cover my eyes and not look until you're done."

No use in being modest now, I said to myself. With a flourish, he put his hands over his eyes. I quickly skinned off my sweater and skirt. I don't wear underwear, just tights. Today my tights were black. As I began to pull them off, I sneaked a look at Bo. His hands were still over his eyes, but his fingers were spread wide so he could peep through them! I was furious.

"Never trust a guitar-player," he said. He was laughing!

After a moment, I decided to laugh too. After all, I'd be showing off plenty to total strangers tonight.

Bo assumed the stance of a doddering old professor and pointed his finger in the air. "If one is to be a dancer," he pompously intoned, "one should be properly dressed. The first thing to do," he placed his hands on my hips, "is to remove these confining tights." He began to roll my tights down my hips.

"Wait! Wait!" I backed away from him rapidly. He followed my across the room still shuffling in his role as the old professor. Faster and faster I backed around as he shuffled. Really fast; I backed into the single dressing-room chair and fell on my butt with a horrible crash.

Ronnie, the club owner, came running. "What's happening here? Bo, what are you up to?"

Bo rolled his eyes in innocence. "I didn't do nothing. Willie Mae here just tripped over the chair. Your dressing room is too damn small. Are you hurt, Willie Mae?" He offered me a hand to help me up.

"No, I'm just fine." We looked at each other and giggled. Ronnie went out, puzzled.

"Now about those tights…" said Bo. We were still laughing. He got in back of me and slowly began rolling my tights down. I wiggled to help him. He rolled carefully, all the way down to my toes. I stepped out of them and he ran his hands slowly back up the sides of my legs. Up my sides, to about my armpits. He then slid them slightly forward and pulled me back against him. He turned me around and kissed me. "Let me lock the door," he said.

I don't know what got into me. I'm not a virgin, but I had never made love to a stranger. And in a dressing room!

He clicked the tiny latch. "We have about an hour," he said. "My band is always late."

"I don't know if I want to," I told him.

"Sure you do," he informed me. He was taking off his shirt. "You're all tense. You don't want to go on stage all tense do you?"

"No, but…" He was taking off his slacks.

"Well, a little lovin' is the best thing for nervous tension." He kicked off his shoes. "Fix you up just fine. You'll dance like a dream. Feel better too." He took off his fire-engine red shorts.

Wow! Did he have a beautiful cock. Long and thick, the kind that stands straight up. That decided me. I just had to have that beautiful piece of meat inside of me. I felt my pussy getting juicy as I looked at it.

"We'll just sit in this chair here," he said. He picked up the chair I had tripped over. One of its legs was broken. It would never stand again. "Maybe if you lean your back against this wall…" he said. I looked at the wall dubiously. It was filthy, and a cockroach scuttled across it as I watched.

"No wall," I said.

Bo looked around quickly. "I have it!" he said. He spread his shirt on the floor in a sweeping gesture and sat on top of it. "Come here and sit on my lap," he said.

I wasn't sure we could manage it. Awkwardly, I sat myself down in his lap. He put his arms around my waist. As I sat down, his enormous prick slid into my hungry pussy. I was a little tight, so he jiggled me up and down on his joint to effect an entrance. Soon he was in up to the hilt. Delicious sensations shot through my groin as he bounced me on to his long pole. When he got all the way into me, we began to rock back and forth. See Saw, Marjorie Daw. Bo's boney butt bouncing on the floor. Every movement stirred unbearable sensations through my middle.

There was a knock on the door. "Fifteen minutes!" hollered Ronnie. He was telling us how long before we had to be on stage.

We huffed and puffed together like a train going up a hill. The floorboards creaked under our motion.

"Ten minutes!" yelled Ronnie outside the door.

Sweat poured off our bodies and mingled in our crotch. My cunt felt like a great pudding being stirred by a master cook.

"Five minutes!"

We were rocking at supersonic speed. My whole body was dissolving in a blur of sensation.

"You're on!"

"YAHOO!" Bo let out an enormous yell as he shot high inside me. I was off in a shower of sparks. I thought I would never stop coming. When I did, we rolled sideways together and untangled in a heap. Bo scrambled into his clothes and I got my G-string into place and climbed into my high heels.   We hit the door at the same instant. Ronnie and Bo's band were waiting outside.

"Hurry up, Willie Mae," said Ronnie. "Get on that platform."

My breasts bounced as I walked bravely into the spotlight. I wasn't nervous anymore.

My First Interview

By Antonia

*(Originally Published in **Kiss** Vol. 1 # 24)*

It takes one to know one. Take, for example, the occasion of my first big interview.

The band had just started to break big. I was going to be interviewed by the top rock magazine. I was kind of scared, because I was in no shape for the interview. I mean, I had been up all night, and to escape the comedown, I had got off again that morning. So there I was, doing the float-walk down the street toward my first big interview.

A nice apartment building in the East 60's. I levitate up the elevator, ring the bell. The door opens.

Fine-looking lady interviewer standing there. Short curly brown hair. Blue eyes framed by blue eyeglasses. Cantaloupe boobs, my favorite kind. Businesslike grey dress.

"Hello, Mr. Breslin," she says, very mannerly. "I'm Lauren. Won't you come in?'

"Please call me Bo," I say. As I do, I look into her eyes. I have this thing about looking in chicks' eyes. A lot of reasons for it, but it's always a good idea. As I look into Lauren's baby blues, a realization hits me: this chick is as high as I am! Her pupils are as big as quarters.

"Care for some meth?" I ask cordially.

"Yes," she says, not dropping a stitch. "I could use a little pick-me-up."

I got out my little vial. She gets out, for Chrissake, a jeweled straw! She snorts the powder in a very ladylike manner, born of long practice. I snort too, less ladylike. We radiate friendliness at each other over the little pile of white powder. "Let me see your hands," she says.

I push them across for inspection. My hands are tremendously oversize from years and years of guitar playing, and this fascinates women. Lauren investigates them as if examining precious jewels, with much interesting finer play. "Now for the interview," she says. Our big eyes shine at one another. "Where were you born Bo?'

"Elgin, Illinois." I take back one of my hands and place it on her jaunty boob. She gives no sign of noticing it.

"How old were you when you started playing guitar?"

"Eleven. I heard some of that old rock & roll stuff and that started me off." Jiggle nice weight of boob in left hand. Take back right hand and start petting her calf. I like the feeling of stockings on a woman's leg. I'm a big tactile man. You need a well-developed sense of touch to play guitar, you know.

"How did you..." My hand creeps higher, and she breaks into a laugh. "Where did you get your nerve?"

"Is that part of the interview?" I ask, all wide-eyed. Then I break up too. The last tension between us dissolves.

96

"Well," says Lauren, "I can always make up the interview, I suppose."

"Sure, you know all the answers anyway." She stands up, laughing, and unzips her secretarial-school dress.

Wow! Underneath the dress is a royal blue French lace bra, matching blue bikini panties and a black garter belt. Panty hose just aren't sexy. She looks much less formidable without her clothes on. In fact, she looks like fun.

"Wow," I articulate, "you keep your talent well-hidden."

"In my line of work it's advisable. I usually want the people around me to keep their minds on business. When I don't... Well, I do alright."

I smile. "Come here." She comes into my arms. I give her my hottest kiss, my tongue probing deep into her mouth. She gives back as good as she gets. I feel my temperature going up. Maybe it's the meth.

I rub up and down her backbone, paying special attention to each vertebra. She purrs up against me like a lady tiger and begins to unbutton my shirt. She unbuttons with one hand and traces a fine line down my chest with the other hand. I don't usually like aggressive women, but she has style. I begin to feel like a pasha as she gently slips me out of my shirt, purring all the while. I'm glad I don't wear undershirts. Makes a much better effect when you come out all at once.

She stands back to admire the effect. She likes it. Pretends to stop there.

"Continue," I say. Silently, she works my belt loose. Unzips my trousers and pulls them down to my ankles. My good old wong almost hits her in the eye as she does this. She pretends to ignore it. Gets to my underwear and stops there. My shorts are purple and she finds that amusing.

"You certainly dress like a rock & roll star," she says.

"Yes, I believe in looking the part." I'm beginning to get impatient. "Do you think you can bear to take them off?"

"I suppose I could force myself... though it might be difficult in your present, er, condition."

We both laughed. The Lauren went back to work, carefully working my shorts down around my heavy joint. I sat down in her big easy chair so she could remove my shoes and socks. Then she came and sat in my lap. I kissed her again and reached behind her to unhook her bra. The fastening on women's underwear used to give me a lot of trouble. But experience has taught me how to work with the damned things. The bra comes off smoothly, loosing lovely coral-tipped titties.

I stand her up to slip her out of her panties. She rubs her sweet, smooth ivory belly against my face, still purring. I dip my tongue into her warm belly button, and kiss a line from her stomach to her pubic hair. Nuzzle around there for a bit while she plays with my hair. Then I stand her up, pushing my joint against her stomach while I kiss her again. She messes my hair and I mess hers back. It's good to find a girl who doesn't mind having her hair messed.

Lauren bends over the chair doggy-fashion. The view of creamy asscheeks and the glimmer of pink slit underneath is extremely attractive. I start to position myself behind her.

"Just a minute," she says. "There's a mirror in here."

A mirror! This girl thinks of everything. Still, I have never before watched myself in action, and I'm curious. I understand it's done in Europe a lot. She leads me to her baby blue bedroom, where an almost full length mirror is mounted on a low table. Her large breasts swing forward as she bends down, leaning her hands on a low table. I take a position behind her, coming face to face with myself in the mirror. Slowly, I begin to rub my tool against the moist entrance to her box, up and down. We keep smiling at ourselves in the mirror.

"I feel funny," I admit. "Like I'm on Candid Camera or something. Can't you turn down the lights or something?"

She can. She is prepared, with a red lamp by the side of her bed. In the red lamp, the scene takes on a seductive glow, like an orgy in Hell.

"Are you satisfied now?" she asks, bending over again. For an answer I ram straight in. She butts her head against the mirror and twists her hips like an Egyptian dancer. I can see her breasts swing in counterpoint, reflected in the wicked red light.

She groans as I press the whole length of my cock into her. She is rapidly losing her cool. I'm glad, because I'm losing mine also. There's a time and a place to be cool, but sex is not it. She puts her legs close together and tightens her passage. I respond with a series of short, swift in-and-outs that leave her gasping for breath. She opens her legs again and moves her hips in a circular motion. I reach around to the front to pinch her breasts. Then I grasp her by the hips and begin directing her motions to just the way I would like them. She plays at resisting me for a while, but it gets to her and she comes along for the ride. I slam her forward and back, driving hard and deep with each stroke. I feel the volcano beginning to build inside me. I can't see the mirror anymore. She begins to yip and squirm in the throes of orgasm, twisting in my grasp. My volcano reaches the top of my head and the pit of my stomach simultaneously, and I explode into a thousand Fourth of Julys.

Lauren gives me her jeweled straw as a memento. Oh, and the interview was good, too. A lot of rock & roll people dread interviews, but not me. You meet some of the nicest people that way.

THROUGH THE WINDOW

By Antonia

This story was never published, but circulated among Antonia's friends. All characters are fictional, of course, and any resemblance to persons living or dead is purely coincidental. Legend has it, however, that when this story was read aloud to a certain musician he laughed until milk came out his nose.

Papa was furious. He has a short temper anyway, and since I've been seeing Bruce, he's been impossible. He doesn't like the idea that Bruce is a musician, and he thinks I should obey him in all things. "You're only 15, young lady," he yells at me, "and you'll do as I say while you're living under my roof." My Mom is even worse. "Behave yourself, Rosie," she's always saying. "No decent man will want to marry you if you ruin your reputation." I don't think they were ever young. When Bruce takes me out driving... ha ha, driving, that's funny... and we park near the beach where you can hear the waves hitting the sand, my nipples actually ache with wanting him to touch them. My Papa won't let me go without a bra, of course, but as soon as I get out of the house I head for a public restroom and take the damned thing off. Bruce thinks that's funny. He likes to watch my breasts jiggle when I walk. Sometimes I think he gets a kick out of it when I put one over on my old man.

Well, tonight the shit hit the fan. We had been parked out on Plum Beach, and my nipples were purple from Bruce kissing and biting 'em. My pussy was all hot and sticky, like a melted Popsicle in the summer sun. I never even let Bruce touch me there, because I knew if I did, I'd be lost. Nights like this, I would go home and cry, I wanted him so much. But I was scared.... scared because the act was so final and, most of all, scared of Papa. I knew I would have to give in some day, though. My own body demanded it, and, as Bruce said, I'm not a little girl any more.

Anyway, we were on the way back, and I wanted an ice cream cone. We drove down the avenue and Bruce parked in front of a candy store and ran inside to get my ice cream. I waited in the car, combing my hair. Suddenly I heard a scandalized, "Well, young lady!" and there was my hatchet-faced Aunt Ethel. She'd recognized Bruce's yellow car, of course. .. everyone in the neighborhood knew it.... so there was no use trying to lie. I swear, that old bitch has a dingleberry for a clit. She couldn't wait to get home and tell Papa. And he finally did it. He locked me in my room.

Well, I climbed into my nightgown, turned on the radio, and cried for a while. After about 45 minutes, I heard a little tap on the door. It was my sister, Sally, bless her soul, asking whether there was anything she could do to help. She's 14 and gets the same kind of heat from Papa I do, so she's sympathetic. I scribbled a note to Bruce, telling him of my awful predicament, and prayed that Sally would find an excuse to get out of the house.

About two and a half hours passed. Thank God I had the radio. I could hear Papa and Mama fuming away in the kitchen, saying, "What are we going to do with that girl?" I was all cried out. The music from the radio washed over me and I started thinking about Bruce. I began stroking my breasts as he had done, pinching my nipples a little bit to make them stand up. Almost without thought, my hand traveled up my nightgown and began stroking the

102

fuzz around my pussy. Just then, there came a light tapping on my bedroom window.

"My God," I thought. "There's someone on the fire escape! I wonder if they saw me." Quietly I crept to the window and pulled back the curtain. There was Bruce, crouching on the fire escape and holding his finger to his lips. I was amazed. We live five stories up. I unlatched my window and let him in. "I used to be a cat burglar," he explained.

I realized that all I was wearing was a nightgown, and I started to get into a robe. "Leave it off," whispered Bruce. I was very aware of Papa in the kitchen. I suddenly wished my nightgown was black, instead of the virginal white number I had on.

"Pack your things," he whispered, "We're gettin' out of here." I started to get my shit together. Bruce followed me around the room, kissing me on the back of the neck and making it hard for me to concentrate. Finally I was packed. I sat down on the bed. Bruce followed, making himself right at home.

"Can't have you running around the streets in your nightie," he whispered, and began to unfasten the top button of my gown. It was the button up night shirt kind.

"Papa," I whispered; "he's in the kitchen, two rooms away."

"Turn your radio up a little." I did. Bruce was grinning from ear to ear. He went back to unbuttoning. I had this scary feeling in the pit of my stomach yet I was excited. He finished unbuttoning, and slowly peeled the nightgown off me. Funny, now that I was naked, I felt no shame. Bruce began to get out of his clothes, making almost no sound. Oh, wow, I thought, it's really going to happen. But it couldn't, not with Papa right there in the kitchen.

"Papa will kill us both," I whispered, almost out loud.

"Shh," said Bruce, and began making little circles around my nipple with his finger. I heard the sounds of Mama and Papa going into their bedroom. Thank God they are used to me leaving my radio on all night. Bruce traced a line from my nipple to my belly button, making little circles all the way. His hot slippery tongue was in my mouth; I felt as if a giant light had gone on inside my pussy, radiating heat and electricity. I shivered whenever he touched me. I saw his cock, long and thick, like a snake in the moonlight. Suddenly, his fingers touched my cunt. I said, "Ooh," and jumped a country mile. He put his hand over my mouth, and he continued to probe deeper with his finger. It felt scary, but good. I opened my legs a bit to let him deeper. "That's right," he whispered in my ear. He put another finger in. I was all squishy. I felt the hot length of his cock against my leg. Will it hurt much, I wondered. I tried to say "Don't hurt me", but his hand was still covering my mouth.

He got on top of me. I looked at his face. He was still smiling. He lowered his body down on mine and I felt the steamy head of his cock at the entrance to my cunt. "Raise your legs up higher," he whispered. I did. The head of his rod slid in, stretching and filling me. It felt like my whole being was contained in my cunt. He moved further in, using short, back-and-forth strokes. I moved back against the bed, afraid now. He put his free hand under my ass and stuck a finger up my asshole. As I moved up, he moved forward and broke through me. I cried out, but his hand over my mouth muffled the sound. Then he was all the way inside me.

He lay still then for a few moments, letting my body get used to the feeling of him filling me up inside. Then he began to move, a long slow stroking motion that made me shudder in time. In a few strokes, the pain stopped and a slow, hazy radiance began to spread out from his cock through the center of my body. I moved my legs up higher to take more of him inside and began, hesitantly, to move with him. "Good, Rosie, that's good," he mumbled into my hair. He began to move faster now, increasing the length of his strokes. I moved with him. It was like dancing.

Suddenly, the bed began to squeak. Bruce switched to long, slow strokes with a sort of twist at the end. I had never imagined anything like that. I could feel his whole body shaking. He was babbling reassuring little nonsense words in my ear. I felt the heat in me rise mp to meet him and I twisted on the end of his cock and exploded up at him, biting his hand. I felt him drive into me with his full weight, his body twisting in impossible arcs.

Slowly, I came back to earth. Bruce was murmuring, "Jesus, Rosie!" over and over in my ear. Unwillingly, we separated. I was amazed that Mama and Papa weren't wide awake by now.

I got some jeans, a T-shirt, and a pair of panties out of my closet. Bruce took them out of my hands and dressed me, slowly, like it was some kind of formal ritual. He even put the shoes on my feet. "You're quite a little wildcat, you know," he whispered, and turned around. There were long scratches on his back where I had clawed him.

"Here we go," he said. "Wave bye-bye." I climbed out to the fire escape after him, leaving behind only the open window and the bloodstained bed.

Transformation of Johnny Push

By Antonia

(Originally published in Crawdaddy, circa 1970)

Thirty-five years after it was written, Antonia considers this a story with a sad ending. I don't.

It was Thursday, and Johnny Push was hopeful.

Every Thursday, Champ Booger came to radio station WACK to hawk his wares. Champ Booger was a dope pusher.

Johnny Push was a disc jockey.

And it was Thursday. Johnny was excited. He was not addicted to anything. He was, he thought, too hip to get strung out. But he liked to get high. He liked it a lot. And nowadays, getting high was exciting. There was a new drug every week, and there was a lot to be said for the old ones. And it had been a tough week.

At 11:00 P.M., Champ Booger walked in, followed closely by three hangers-on. He was prompt. At his prices, he should be. But his quality was as high... as high as his prices.

Champ spent a few minutes glad-handing, then got down to business.

"Brand new, Johnny," he said. "Called Aces High. You just swallow it... no messy shooting up or anything. Twenty minutes later ya got a transcendental experience. Way stronger than LSD or anything. It puts ya where ya always wanted to go."

"How much?" Johnny was dubious of transcendental experiences, ever since he got the horrors on STP.

"Well, thirty dollars a cap… but since you're such a high-class customer…"

That did it. Johnny could never resist a bargain. "I'll take two." He counted out forty dollars from the wad in his pocket. "And give me an ounce of grass." Some money changed hands.

"Don't take 'em both at the same time," Champ chuckled. "Yer liable to go to the moon. Har, har!"

"Happy landin's," Champ glad-handed out, trailed by his retinue.

This business was conducted during the course of a rather long record, which Johnny had cued in for the purpose. He still had 45 minutes of his show to do. Conscientiously, he did not take the Aces High during the show. At midnight, his show went off the air. At 12:01, he swallowed both capsules of Aces High.

At 12:21, Johnny Push saw God.

"Saw" is perhaps the wrong word. "Perceived" is better. He became aware of the unity of all things, and of an all-wise, all-good Force which was controlling that unity, which, in fact, had invented that unity for its own pleasure.

"Omigawd," said Johnny.

108

Ike, Johnny's number one engineer, was an old hand at drug crises. He moved in sympathetically. "You OK, Johnny?"

Johnny was nothing if not cool. "Fine, Ike, just fine. Stomach acting up a bit from this new stuff, that's all." He had broken out in a cold sweat. "Glad its time to go home."

"Everybody is." Ike stuck to grass and beer and considered himself well off. "Well, good night."

"Good night." Johnny pulled on his sports jacket and went into the street. Finding himself alone, he stopped to check.

It hadn't gone away. God was still there.

Of course God was still there, Johnny thought with annoyance, and I'm still stoned out of my gourd. Shouldn't have taken both caps but, since I did, I'll sit back and enjoy my trip. It will all blow over tomorrow.

He felt no other side effects, but took a taxi to his apartment just in case. The driver was talkative. Johnny had always considered talkative cabbies an affront. And Johnny had a short temper.

He framed an appropriately cutting remark.

He was just about to deliver it when he became aware of the infinite sadness of all around him. The very air wept for his misguided soul. At the same time, he felt a brotherhood with the driver, a kinship closer that he had ever felt for his own family.

Johnny held his tongue. Indeed, he began to answer in a civil manner, and soon found himself involved in a long discussion of the merits of various baseball teams.

They came to his building. Getting out of the cab, Johnny felt pretty good. Martha, his wife, was sleeping when he came in. He was careful not to wake her.

To his surprise, he had no trouble falling asleep and no unpleasant physical symptoms.

The next morning It was still there. Johnny looked in the bathroom mirror and saw his own face.

Johnny was a brave man. He greeted it cheerfully. "Good morning, Ever-Present Fullness," he said.

In the bedroom, Martha was fumbling into wakefulness. "Who you talking to?" she mumbled.

"God," he shouted back. Martha laughed. They joked a lot between themselves.

"Well, tell him to do something about the plumber... He didn't come yesterday."

Johnny thought for a moment. "About the plumber…" he began quietly, hesitantly.

He perceived an answer. "God says all in the order of things," he hollered out to the bedroom.

"Oh." Martha laughed again. She laughed a lot. It was one of the reasons he had married her. Lately it had begun to annoy him.

He dressed carefully and ate his brunch. Although it was early afternoon, he was going to the studio. Some record company wanted an album plugged, and that meant Girls.

He arrived at the studio in high spirits. Girls. Martha was a good kid but, he believed, a man needed a little something on the side to sort of keep his hand in.

It was a big promotional deal. Three were about seven girls in the studio all giggling, wiggling, and full of fun. An adorable fluffy blonde made her way over to him. "Hi," she said in a throaty, giggly voice. "You're Johnny Push. I seen your picture in the newspaper." I'm Lola."

"Hi, Lola." He slid his hand down her back. Lower, lower, until he almost accidentally brushed the curve of her buttocks. As he made contact with that well-rounded portion of her anatomy, Lola's life story appeared to him in a blinding flash. She was a dope addict, forced into prostitution by her need for drugs. She loathed men.

Johnny felt a deep, abiding sadness for her and for the other girls in the room. It totally unmanned him.

He slipped $30 to Lola – all the money in his pocket – and shrugged into his sports jacket.

Ike spotted him. "Hey, where you going?" said the engineer. "The party's just beginning."

"I'm through with parties," said Johnny without thinking.

Ike laughed. "What are you, turning into some kind of fuckin' saint?"

"Yeah," said Johnny sadly, going out the door.

Why Women Don't Play the Didgeridoo

An unpublished story by Antonia *(courtesy of Maggie Roche)*
This may be more a shaggy dog joke than a story, but I like it!

The didgeridoo is the basic Australian wind instrument, which gives Australian music its characteristic sound. The greatest didgeridoo player who ever lived was a woman I shall call Susie-Q, because I can't spell her Australian name. When Susie-Q blew her didgeridoo, the very spirits of the stones would get up and dance.

Susie-Q was unusual in another way – she preferred the love of her own sex. Specifically, she lusted after a young maiden called Possum. She befriended the girl, and eventually invited Possum to her home. She told the young girl that she would show her the secrets of married people. Possum's innocent curiosity got the better of her, and that evening she came to Susie-Q's hut.

Susie-Q brought forth her large, elaborately-carved didgeridoo. She place one end in her mouth and instructed Possum to remove her loincloth and sit down firmly on the other end. Then she began to play.

Like most musicians, Susie-Q liked to play at night, and this was fortunate, because nobody suspected that Possum was frequently (and delightedly) seated at the far end. But there came a time for Possum to be married.

There was a big wedding feast and then the newlyweds went off to begin their life together. Possum's husband made love to her gently and with great skill. When it was over, Possum smiled at him and said, "That's all well and good, but I *can't wait* for you to get out your didgeridoo!" A few questions, and the whole story came out.

113

Susie-Q ran for her life, leaving her precious didgeridoo behind. She never was found, but from that day forward, women have been forbidden to play the didgeridoo.

CANDLE MAGIC FOR BEGINNERS

by Antonia

This appeared in **Crawdaddy** *around 1970, when Antonia was deeply into magic: with her dramatic, dazzling-white hair, she certainly looked the part. Some years later, when our daughter was born, Antonia gave her a little-girl purse, very cute. Inside she had placed some High John the Conqueror root to protect her from evil. She still swears by the stuff... Antonia also wrote an article for* **Crawdaddy** *titled "Sex and Drugs" which offers an experienced perspective on how a wide variety of drugs affect sexual experience, which I have chosen not to include here.*

Candle burning to achieve special purposes has been going on for a long time. So much for the historical aspects.

Now for the practical aspects. Practical? Yes. Candle burning helps a person to focus his concentration on what he wants, and enough concentration can move mountains.

Candles of different colors have different significances, and there are various oils to dress the candles that will increase their efficiency. These oils are usually found in Negro [sic] or Spanish-speaking neighborhoods, where religious candle burning is commonplace. (In the Spanish-speaking neighborhoods, the labels on the oils will, of course, be in Spanish, so be prepared.) There are often incenses to go along with the oils. Most of the names of the oils are self-explanatory (Money-Drawing, Attraction, etc.), but some will require interpretation.

Dressing a candle, or putting oil on it, is done from center to top, and then from center to bottom, without crossing the two. This is called observing the laws of polarity. Fail to observe the laws of polarity & you risk dabbling in black magic. Dabbling in black magic is a bad idea because magic comes back on you three times, in some way. If you're not sure, don't do it. Magic requires a sense of responsibility. There are altogether too many half-assed "magicians" around.

I suppose the easiest way to explain candle burning is to explain the significance of each color candle, and list some of the oils used with it.

White candles are the most commonly used. White symbolizes purity, and the forces of good. White candles are often used with Holy Oil. A white candle & some Frankincense (or a white candle dressed with Frankincense Oil) is a good "thank you" to the Powers that Be for a spell that works or a prayer that is answered.

Black candles, dressed with Confusion Oil, symbolize the conquest of evil. These are best used in combination with a white candle which is larger than the black candle, symbolizing the ascendancy of good over evil.

Grey is for uncrossing. A person or thing is said to be "crossed" if they keep having bad luck. A whole house can be crossed. This is often the result of someone's bad thoughts toward the crossed person. A grey candle with Uncrossing Oil will usually do the trick here.

Red is used for love, sex, health, victory in war, and all matters concerning the body. Cleopatra Oil on a red candle is an effective but rather sexual love charm. St. Michael Incense burned alongside a red candle is said to protect men at war or engaged in any sort of battle. Lovers Oil & Attraction Oil will make a gentler love charm. Radiant Health Oil will help in a time of sickness.

Green pertains to money, jobs, and the material world. When used with Five Circles Oil, it can often help to resolve an uncertainty connected with your career. Gamblers of all types often use green candles with Fast Luck or Black Cat Oil -- useful for all kinds of people who take chances or play games.

Gold is the color of attraction or success. Success Oil is an obvious choice with this. Also used is Lodestone Oil, which will draw things you want in your direction. Attraction Oil is for attracting certain conditions (not a love charm). Seven Powers Oil is to increase your personal charisma.

Purple has always symbolized power. A very strong spell to increase your personal power involves a purple candle dressed with Seven Powers Oil burned alongside some High John Conquering Incense. Also any oil containing High John the Conqueror root.

Blue is the color of the spirit world & the occult. Also the mind. Spirit Oil on a blue candle is supposed to be pleasing to the spirit world & make the spirits more helpful toward you. Peaceful Home Incense burned near a blue candle provides a tranquil atmosphere. Indian Guide Oil will sometimes induce a specific spirit to help you in your occult efforts. Good ol' Five Circles Oil will often help to pull off a spell. Five Circles Oil is about the best oil I know. Its uses are limited only by the imagination of the user.

Yellow is the color of revelation. Try Seventh Heaven Oil or Seven Powers.

Brown is associated with Saint Anthony, who hears the prayers of sweethearts. A candle for romantic love. Write the name of the beloved on a slip of paper, place under the candle, and dress with Saint Anthony's or Lovers Oil. Best done for seven days in a row.

Orange is for dreams or revelations. Seventh Heaven Oil for dreams. Concentration Oil for concentration, Five Circles Oil for surprising & interesting results.

Pink for joy, with Seventh Heaven Oil.

There are also specially shaped candles available sometimes. A Seven Knots candle is shaped like seven balls piled one on top of the other & is burned one knot per day, providing a very strong spell. Red for love, green for money, black for uncrossing.

A very powerful love charm is a figure of a man or woman. These come in black, white or red. One of the love oils is used, or sometimes Commanding or Controlling Oil. This makes a very strong binding spell & should be used with great caution, as it borders on black magic. I'm not sure about this one, morally.

A strong uncrossing charm is a wax image of the Devil, with Confusion Oil on it.

A candle in the shape of a cat, with Seven Powers Oil, Master Oil, or Power Oil, is said to increase your powers.

Each sign of the zodiac has a different floral essence, and these put on a candle will help to focus on a particular person of that sign.

The House of Candles & Talismans on Stanton Street in Manhattan is one source of these oils & candles. The Compleat Enchanter in Los Angeles can also supply you with the necessary paraphernalia.

Good luck.

Bird Poetry and Songs

Over the last decade or so Antonia has had a passionate interest in birds, participating actively in bird societies. Her beloved cockatiel, Tommy Tune, moved to Florida with her and, while she cannot keep him with her in her assisted-living facility, he still lives nearby. These poems and song were published by SQUAWK, the newsletter of the Big Apple Bird Association.

Mr. Twinkle's Song

The grey of your breast
puts the moonlight to shame.
Your wings are the green
of the new leaves in spring.
Your dear little beak
is an apricot flame.
And you are the heart
of the song that I sing.
We're two different species
I know this is true.
But nevertheless
I dream only of you.

Scooter's Reply

Is that you on my cage again?
Is that you coming in my door?
I don't recall inviting you
To perch with me. And furthermore,
You'd better pack your wings and go
Unless you want to lose a Toe.

Bite My Gypsy Earrings

Background to Song:

A couple of years ago, my friends bought a cockatiel for their 7-year-old daughter, & I just went over to look at it. Someone plunked the bird onto my shoulder, & my life changed forever. Sadly, Yellow did not live very long, but the wonder I felt when he first perched on my shoulder is still with me, & will probably remain for the rest of my life. This is a song, though the music has not been written down...

This song is dedicated to the memory of Yellow Crunchy Button, a cockatiel

Verse 1

I felt your heart beat rapidly

Warm feathers on my shoulder

I was confused - what made me think

that you'd be so much colder?

You took a chance - well, so did I

Amazing how we grew

The way you got so "tall" to me

I got so high on you

Chorus:

I wore my Gypsy earrings just for you

Don't you love the way they sparkle

like the sunlight on the dew?

I barely got to know you

I had so much to learn

You slipped right past me

while my back was turned.

Well things have changed - you made a change

Much more than I expected.

My little crunchy button friend

On this I stand corrected

And nothing's ever lived in vain

And nothing's gone to waste

And how I'd love once more to see

Your silly little face

F E E P

This poem is dedicated to Cockatiel owners.

I try to keep his wings clipped,

But the mischief doesn't stop.

He now goes underneath things

Since he can't fly up on top.

He's underneath my sofa

He's underneath my feet

He's underneath my table

Yelling, "FEEP! FEEP! FEEP!"

Oh somewhere there's a cockatiel

Of feminine design

Who wonders "Will I ever meet

the boyd who will be mine?"

I'll say, "Don't worry, sugar,

You could find him in your sleep.

He's underneath my table

Yelling, "FEEP! FEEP! FEEP!"

Chapter Six: Selected Lyrics

Antonia's overall creative output was enormous, but her songs – her lyrics in particular – are inarguably her crowning achievement. No one, including Antonia herself, can say for certain how many sets of lyrics she composed. Many exist only on scraps of notebook paper, others are irretrievably lost. What follows is a selection of her best-known, most cherished, and finest lyrics, both recorded and unrecorded.

Love made a liar out of me

(Antonia) To hear Antonia singing this in a strong, sly and sexy voice on a demo tape made in the late 1970's is to grieve that such a marvelous song was never recorded...

(Cause it was) love made a liar out of me
Poor me!
I'm just too kind to be true!

You saw me talking with my used-to-be the other day
And you made up your mind before I even had a chance to have my say
You sure got one suspicious mind!

He said he'd die if he could never see me anymore
How could I turn him down when it was such a little thing he asked me for?
You sure got one suspicious mind!

(Cause it was) love made a liar out of me
Poor me!
I'm just too kind to be true!

No, I will not give back that Cadillac he gave me
Cause it would tear him all apart if I refused his generosity
You sure got one suspicious mind!

You should be glad I got a tender heart that lives to please
Just give me love and any other thing you got and skip the third degree
You sure got one suspicious mind!

(Cause it was) love made a liar out of me
Poor me!
I'm just too kind to be true, oh yeah
I'm just too kind to be true!

To a snake with love

(Antonia) One of several songs Antonia wrote about Weber. A guy named Bazza out in Portland does a remarkable version of this in a very slow tempo.

The first time that I saw you, you appeared to be so strange
Not like other people that I knew
You seemed to cast a spell before you everywhere you went
And everything you touched I saw anew
Not knowing if you cast your spell for evil or for good
But wanting to be part of you in any way I could
I let you hypnotize me like a snake does with a bird
I lost myself and found myself in you

I never asked you questions 'bout what you did or why
You never would have answered anyway
You had a certain sureness of yourself and all you did
A game that no-one else but you could play
You told me what to do and I obeyed you willingly
Your fire lit my darkness, and you showed me what to see
I need no explanation, words are meaningless to me
I lost myself and found myself in you

And loving you has come to mean an acceptance so complete
I could not turn back if I wanted to
My life is laid before you like the prism of a jewel
and you are like the sunlight blazing through
Cast up upon the beach of my own vagaries and fears
I could not see the sunlight through the prison of my tears.
But now when you are close to me the morning sun appears
I lost myself and found myself in you

HooDoo Bash

(Antonia) One of Antonia's best known and most beloved songs. "Singing Bear," of course, is Antonia herself.

Down at the station at one in the morning
There's a trainload of strangers that just hit town
One has a top hat and one has a falcon
And although they've just arrived they know their way around

Out to a house at the edge of the town
They're bringing Thunderbird wine and a pound of hash
Come on along if you're one of the people
'cause we're going to get the spirit down at the HooDoo Bash!

All them wizards from the south
Came up special for the big turn-out
Golden Blossom, Singing bear
They're gonna have a party and they just don't care!

Fasten your seat-belts, let down your hair
Because tonight is the night we've been waiting for
People in trances and African dances
Because another kind of life is waiting behind that door

We got supplies that will last for a week
So there ain't nothing to stop us until we crash
When we have kids we can tell them the story
'bout the night we got the spirit down at the HooDoo Bash!

Magic mushrooms from Singing Bear
Indian visions that'll curl your hair
Golden Blossom said she'd bake
Her dandelion wine and morning-glory cake

Tell all your friends that you've gone out of town
And be prepared to go out of your natural mind
We're going to rise when the sun's going down
And when the spirit starts to move you'll never know what you'll find

If you're afraid, then you'd better stay home
Because there's no turning back once the dice are cast
Lovers or strangers, we all go through changes
When we get that good old spirit down at the HooDoo Bash!

125

I disremember quite well

(Antonia) Gee, I wonder who this one was written about? I have always imagined Hurley singing it...

You'll pardon me if I act strange
But we've been out of touch
I know that time is on your side
But time can do so much
Are you still makin' it with time?
I disremember quite well

Yes, I can see as I come close
Time has been good to you.
Just for a moment's truth
You almost had the face I knew
But now of course it's not for real
I disremember quite well

I used to know you when you turned
Your water into wine
You played the shell game with yourself
And won it every time
But where are you going to keep your prize?
I disremember quite well

I used to walk on the water too
And float above the sand
And hang the stars like diamonds
From my outstretched greedy hands
But I've forgotten how that game goes.
I disremember quite well

And did you ever do whatever
Thing it is you're for
Or does an old idea like that
Have meaning anymore?
The "maybe" that I loved has gone – but where?
I disremember quite well

Going to See the King

(Antonia) This is my very favorite song by Antonia. I used to perform it in the early eighties, and hope to again in the years ahead. If it is not an overtly religious song (I think it is; Antonia would likely disagree) it is certainly spiritual. And hopeful. And uplifting. And a whole lot better than most of the crap being sung in churches these days.

I wait by peaceful waters
My ship is drawing near
My soul is free; the things I see
Are obvious and clear
Are obvious and clear
Are obvious and clear Whoa-o-oh

chorus
Come brighter day
Take me away
I'll sail across blue skyways
Come brighter day
Take me away
I'm going to see the king

(chorus)

Cold death is my ship's captain
He holds no fears for me
He'll steer me far
Beyond the stars
'til paradise I'll see
'til paradise I'll see
'til paradise I'll see, whoa-o-oh

(chorus sung twice)

Don't cry for me, my loved ones
My ship will take me home
Though life is gone
My soul lives on
I do not sail alone
I do not sail alone
I do not sail alone, whoa-o-oh
(chorus)

Sentimental Song

(Antonia) Another one about Weber. She wrote enough songs about their complex relationship to constitute a "Weber Suite."

I used to have a friend
No one you'd care to meet
Sometimes we'd pretend
I could keep him off the street
I have a peaceful life ahead of me

Though we had funny ways
We knew each other's tastes
We would fight for days
It filled up all the space
I have a peaceful life ahead of me

Now I have no more friend
We just ran out of luck
Would I do it again?
Not for a million bucks
I have a peaceful life ahead of me

Behind the Red Door

(Antonia/McClean) This song was, regularly performed by Corona at clubs in and around Portland, Oregon. She tried not to sing it in front of children.

Here below the Mexican border, there's no law and order
So we can have fun.
There's a red lantern hung over the doorway, we'll do it your way.
Just give us your gun.
Fun, fun, just give us your gun.

If you're an outlaw we'll keep you well hidden, nothing's forbidden
Behind the red door.
Lovely Maria will serve you tequila, but if you want to feel her
It's ten pesos more.
More, more, its ten pesos more.

We'll tempt you to ramble, we'll tempt you to gamble;
We'll lose all the money you stole.
We know you have aces in all the wrong places
But we have that ace in the hole.
A whole lot of ace in the hole.

So come right on in, we don't care where you've been,
We're not shocked by your sin
Cause we've seen it before.
Take off your sombrero and let down your hair-o
And no one will care-o behind the red door.
Yes, no one cares behind the red door.

Crying in the Shower

(Lyrics: Wollheim/Bingham/Stampfel/Antonia. Music: Stampfel/Antonia)
As I recall, this was a group effort written around the table over an Italian meal.

Chorus
Crying in the Shower, no one overhears
While my lonely tears go drifting down the drain
From the sewer to the sea
My tears flow endlessly
Crying in the shower

I wake up in the morning like morning people do
An icebag on my head and an aspirin or two
I wish there was an aspirin to cure a broken heart
I wish my morning shower didn't make my teardrops start

(chorus)

Lily's busy counting, she thinks she's four days late
Nathan's whistling loudly, Nathan listens great
Everybody's doing the things they always do
I'm staying in the shower until my crying's through

(chorus)

I step out of the bathroom, a smile upon my face
I have the strength and courage to face the human race
My sorrow's on its way now from sewer to the sea
I think I'll buy a six-pack and sit and watch tv

(chorus)

Focke-Wulf Blues

(Messerschmitt/Antonia) "Messerschmitt" was a guy named John, the Rounders roadie around 1970. I blame Peter for introducing Antonia to the virtues of WWI fighter planes. Sex, of course, she discovered on her own.

Waitin at the airport for my pilot to come by
Waitin for the time when I can jump into the sky
Tired of being grounded, I want to get up high
Yonder comes my pilot
Now you're gonna see me fly

Roaring down the runway you can hear my engine yell
Heading for the battle like a bat right out of hell
Pilot at the throttle, he thinks he's quite a man
But without me underneath him
He'd be in no man's land

Chasin down the bombers, I can shoot down every one
Spitfires and Thunderbolts all fall before my gun
I'm a Focke-Wulf fighter, listen to my engine sing
Ain't nobody that can catch me
When I am on the wing

I don't care who flies me, I ain't no one's fuckin dog
I can lose pursuers just like rolling off a log
I can out-maneuver any plane you'll ever see
Just as long as I am flying
It's all the same to me

I will fly on any side that keeps me in the air
Who will be my pilot, well I can't say that I care
Cause I was born for battle, yeah I'm a killer plane
And I never will rest easy
Til I go down in flames

Byzantine Rock

(Antonia/Stampfel) I got this one from Peter, complete with chords. It has never been performed, but he can still sing every note.

Do I hear the voice of my Byzantine queen
Who calls from a country that never quite was
Across an abyss with my fears in between
And is she in my mind, or am I in hers?
The chasm between us is deeper than sin
Its walls are a mountain that's turned inside-out
By something that wants me to stay where I've been
And spends its life plotting against me, do doubt

Bridge – ragtime
Scheming Loretta and Plotting Frank
And all of those others you never quite see
They're tapping my phone and they're watching my house
And I've got a feeling they're out to get me
Meanwhile, back in Byzantium
The moon is always full and red
And someone that I almost know
Watches the inside of my head

My queen is as dark as the midnight sky
I've not seen her face, but I know she is fair
She whispers a secret that may be a lie
Or may be the truth, if in truth she is there
For women are born knowing how to deceive
And men are a greedy and treacherous lot
And I am the only one I can believe
Unless I should find myself part of the plot

Oh, WOE

(Antonia) *Antonia has notebooks filled with both completed and partially completed songs. Peter and Betsy have several similar notebooks. This song, complete with chords, was obviously started, set aside, and finished at a later date. It is not marked as such, but the first stanza is clearly the chorus.*

Oh Woe, Oh Woe
Oh, what a way to go
Derailed by all the people I connect with
And every time I think I'm hooked up
Someone disappears
Why do they make it so damn hard for me
To join the human race?

Once I had me a lover
Who brought me the moon on a tray
He wouldn't let me lift a finger
I finally felt so useless that I had to go away

One time on vacation
I tried to visit the Queen
They told me I was too ugly
They said my face would scare her and they wouldn't let me in

Once I called up the devil
Tried to sell him my soul
He wouldn't make me no offers
He said he had no use for it, if all the truth be told

Once I had me a vision
That gave me a moment of hope
When I told the world of my vision
They threw me into jail, they said I must be taking dope

The following three songs are all taken from notebooks filled with lyrics. I am not certain if Antonia regarded them as completed, and doubt that any of them have been publicly performed. Two of them include chords, so clearly she wrote the music for them as well.

One Star
(Antonia)

My love is ever-changing
Time will not pass it by
You always know I love you
You never know why
You never know why

A living thing, my love is
It doesn't want to die
There's something to be gained here
And reason to try
And reason to try

I've given up on dreaming
The cost became too high
But see, when you look closely
One star in my eye
One star in my eye

New Old-Timey Bright Green Blues
(Antonia) A second verse to this song got lost along the way.

Hey there, Leon Russell
A fellow gotta hustle
To do his thing just half as good as you
And when you do it
You really sail right thru it
You make it look too easy to be true
If each of us could have your gifts
For just a little while
This dreary world we're living in would
Have a lot more style
You got back so good
Cuz you understood
You play them new old timey bright green blues

134

Hoodoo I Owe my Body to?

(Antonia)

Hoodoo Hoodoo
Hoodoo I owe my body to?
If someone else wants to lay a claim
Let them share in the upkeep and the pain

I was born through no fault of my own
And commenced to live my life
I soon found the world was a hard place
Full of pain and strife

People coming at me from all sides
Telling me what is right
But if I ain't hurting no one but myself
Tell me, who gives them the right?

The Mo-mo song

(Antonia) Antonia was particularly invested in having this song included. I did not know it, but fortunately Maggie Roche had a copy. It was originally intended to be included on **Have Moicy**! *but the guys just couldn't handle such blatant female sexual empowerment. This song will tell you a lot about Antonia's adolescence. And adulthood.*

Most people think I am a good girl
I don't tell lies or fight or steal
I get good marks in all my schoolwork
And clean my plate at every meal
But I have got a wicked secret
That I must never, never tell
A thing I do sometimes with Rosie
And sometimes when I'm by myself.

chorus
Gonna let the Mo-Mo come and get me
Gonna let the Mo-Mo come and get me
I can't be a good girl anymore
Wonder what it feels like to be dead?
Hope I don't get scared and wet the bed
When I hear that monster at my door.

There is a monster called the Mo-Mo
That's what my best friend Rosie said
He comes at night and peeps in windows
When little girls are in their beds
He sees what everyone is doing
And he can get in anywhere
He comes and eats the naughty children
Who like to touch themselves down there.

My mother says Down There is nasty;
It doesn't even have a name
And we must always keep it covered
To think about it is a shame
But me and Rosie got to wondering
If all we girls are built the same
So one day we just took our pants off
And played a little piggy game

136

This is an awful thing to tell you
But that place feels so good to touch
I think that's what it must be made for
And I like mine so very much
I'd rather let the Mo-Mo eat me
Than make believe I hate that place
So come and get me, you big monster:
I hope you like the way I taste!

Call it Solitude

(Antonia/Ito) One of several sets of lyrics Antonia wrote where Genji Ito supplied the melody.

In my private mood
What I feel is nothing but loneliness
Call it solitude
Shining times alone when my life is blessed
When my mind and body make no demands
And I'll sing this song so you will understand.

In my private mood
What I feel does not mean I love you less
Call it food for thought
Sorting out the right from the wrong, at best
There are places I would like to explore
There are treasures, they are waiting in store

Bridge
I will return a richer man
Rich with the gold of my own hands
Let my spirit fly

In my private mood
I will reap the harvest and plant the seed
Call it solitude
I must be alone when I feel the need
Please don't worry, for when the time is through
I'll remember and I will come to you

Reasons to be Fearful

There was a song called "Reasons to be Cheerful" playing incessantly on the radio and, as often happened, Antonia broke into extemporaneous parody...

Feel the dentist drilling, losing a filling
Psychopathic killing, income tax
Nitrate in your bacon, feel your floor shaking
Taking a vacation when you can't relax
Mother of a bear cub, Indian war club
Roaches in the bathtub, snakes all curled
Running from a landslide, caught in a rip tide
Jeans rip up the backside, moon the world

Teacher caught you cheating, taking a beating
Going trick or treating late at night
All the kids are hipper, mouse in your slipper
Freaky acid tripper, does he bite?
Daddy caught you smoking, TV is broken
Pushin' and a pokin', standing in line
Drive without a license, writing this nonsense
Hare Krishna incense, doing time

Nothing in your stash box, room smells of gym sox
Cold-turkey detox, land on your head
Whiskey wrecks your liver, Indian giver
Deli won't deliver, wish you were dead
Breathing the pollution, no absolution
Part of the solution, went down the drain
Ain't no use in runnin', I ain't funnin'
Know tomorrow's coming, ain't that a shame?

Scooter's Song

*(Antonia) Antonia called very active children "Scooters" and loved them dearly,
so long as they were not visiting her apartment and breaking her stuff. The
same term describes adults with boundless energy and enthusiasm.*

You showed up on my stoop one day
With your overalls inside out
You said Big Kenny did you in
But that's nothing to cry about
Asked if you could hang out for awhile
Till Big Kenny got tired and went away
Never thought I could learn so much
From a kid when I let you in that day

Chorus
Sunlight in your eyes, a surprise in your pocket
"Wee-wee" sounded dumb, so we called it a rocket
Where you going to, Scooter pal?
Sneakers on your feet and a startled expression
Devil dogs to eat and another damn question
Where you going to, Scooter pal?

You were back in a day or two
Had a fight with your mom and dad
There were questions you couldn't ask
There were parts of you that were bad
Had to straighten my own head out
When I figured out how to answer you
"What's those pillow on ladies' chests?"
That's something to answer you straight and true.

Took you down to the zoo last week
Watched the animals shit and pee
Took you home to a nice warm tub
You made animal sounds for me
What's inside people's heads, you asked
That the animals never get to know?
What's inside people's heads, I asked
That they bury and never get to show?

139

That Belly I idolize

(Antonia/Stampfel) What's not to love about a belly?

Some folks say you don't do right
You're mean in the morning' gone all night
But I don't care.
You got that belly
I idolize

Your hair is long, your waist is trim
You own three quarters of IBM
But I don't care.
You got that belly
I idolize

When you and your belly go to town
The dogs start howling and the shops close down
And everybody lines up
On the far side of Main Street
And watches you walk towards them
Your belly is firm, your belly is sweet
It ain't no girdle, its good red meat
The kind I like.
You got that belly
I idolize

If You Want to be a Bird

*(Antonia) First recorded on **Moray Eels** and again on **Last Round**, this is
Antonia's most widely-heard song. It is no more about drugs than, say, "Lucy
in the Sky with Diamonds" is.*

If you want to be a bird
Why don't you try a little flying
There's no denying
It gets you high
Why be shackled to your feet
When you've got wings you haven't used yet
Don't wait for heaven
Get out and fly

Just glide there
Through the clear air
Making figure eights
Thought the pearly gates
Where the soul and the universe meet

If you want to be a bird
It won't take much
To get you up there
But when you come down
Land on your feet

God, what am I doing here?

(Antonia) Antonia recalls this as a song she wrote, or began to write, while still a teen. Whether that is accurate or not, it is a haunting song.

The cold wind from space
Is blowing in my face
God, what am I doing here?
I wish I was a cat
So I'd know where it's at
Sure has been a funny year

The dripping of my faucet
Puts a rhythm to the night
I walk around in time with it
My footprints would be white
I touch my body, seeing
I'm still a human being
God, what am I doing here?

The shoreline disappears
The view goes on for years
Time is like an endless sea
I row my little boat
And try to stay afloat
Waiting for eternity

The music all around me
Puts an order to my day
But I am rarely high enough
To see the world that way
Oh please give me a sign
Is all this nonsense mine?
God, what am I doing here?

Snappin' Pussy

(Stampfel/Antonia) A raucous parody of the novelty hit, "Peanut Butter."
Wherever the boundaries of good taste may lie, this song is on the other side of
said boundaries. This is the full and proper version, never recorded. Add your
own "snappin' pussy" to the last two verses…

Fatty, daddy's got a favorite summertime treat
(Snappin', Snappin' pussy!)
Watchin' young lady snappin' pussy boogie down the street
(Snappin', Snappin' pussy!)
Fatty Daddy loves 'em when they're supple and young
 (Snappin' snappin' pussy!)
Daddy spends his lifetime on the bottom rung
 (Snappin' snappin' pussy!)
I like snappin' pussy
Creamy snappin' pussy
Crunchy snappin' pussy too

Even when they're busy on the latest bust
(Snappin', Snappin' pussy)
Every FBI man just tremblin' with lust
(Snappin', Snappin' pussy!)
Back in the office, scribbling on the blotter
(Snappin', Snappin' pussy!)
Every single one of them is horny for their daughter
(Snappin', Snappin' pussy!)
Well I like snappin' pussy
Creamy snappin' pussy
Crunchy snappin' pussy too

Fat black cat bites in New Orleans
Fatty Daddy likes them in their early teens
Fatty Daddy never, never gonna learn
Daughter does the boogaloo to watch him burn

Fatty Daddy waking in a hotel room
Told the clerk his daughter's gonna be there soon
Never gonna go to that hotel again
Whole hotel's full of dirty old men

143

Black Bottom

(Antonia/ Weber/Stampfel) Certainly a Black Bottom Woman lives in Antonia's heart...

If you go down to Black Bottom
Put your money in your shoe
Cause them Black Bottom Women
Got them Back Bottom blues
Oh, good mama, papa got them
Black Bottom blues

Once I knew a preacher
Preached the Bible through and through
He went down to Black Bottom
Now his preaching days are through
Oh, good mama, papa got them
Black Bottom blues

God don't like no ugly
He say "Girl your home's in hell"
I don't play me no dozen
I just like to count to twelve
Oh, good mama, papa's got them
Black Bottom blues

Hooker in Black Bottom
Saying "Thank you, call again"
"If you want that A-200
I'm gonna have to charge you ten"
Oh, good mama, papa's got them
Black Bottom blues

If you got down to Black Bottom
Put your money in your shoe
Cause them Black Bottom Women
Got them Black Bottom blues

Livin' Off the Land

(Stampfel/Antonia) Antonia loves the world of nature, really. She simple prefers it to be on her television or displayed at the zoo.

chorus
Hey bop ba, livin' off the land
Hey bop ba, livin' off the land
Hey bop ba, livin' off the land
Isn't nature grand

Come with me, Samantha Lee
Forsake them city lights
Come to where ya can breathe the air
And see the stars at night

(chorus)

I will build a teepee
You will cook a stew
We'll do all them country things
That country people do

(chorus)

We will have a pet raccoon
Maybe we'll have two
If you ask me real nice
I'll let them sleep with you

(chorus)

Making love is sweeter still
Underneath the sky
Listening to the woodland sounds
Lying in the pines

(chorus)

Take-Off Artist Song

(Stampfel/Antonia)   Inspired by an actual robbery (rip-off, take-off) of their apartment, this song vented a little bit of anger and hostility...

Have you heard about the take-off creep
Who just came into town
Only thing that gets him off
Is burning people down
Gonna bring that take-off artist down!

Don't believe in property
Thinks we all should share
Everywhere he goes
Things seem to vanish into air
Gonna bring that take-off artist down!

Every night he's going round
Playin' his game of lost and found
When I get that take-off clown
Gonna bring that take-off artist down!

Gonna do him dirty
I ain't gonna stop
Gonna use his brain
As my private Johnny-mop
I'm gonna bring that take-off artist down!

If I get too lazy
To pound him into mush
I'll put Draino in his duji
And wait for him to rush
Gonna bring him down

Every night he's going round, round
Playin' his game of lost and found
When I get that flower child
Gonna bring that take-off artist down!

Gonna make him crawl
On his belly like a slug
Pound him into dust and
Sweep him under the rug!

146

Gonna bring that take-off artist down!

When there's nothing left of him
That mortal man can save
I'll piss upon his tombstone and
Desecrate his grave
Gonna bring that take-off artist down

Every night he's going round
Playin' his game of lost and found
When I get that take-off clown
Gonna bring that take-off artist down

I'll follow his immortal soul
Down to the depths of Hell
Watch the devil roast him
Cheer each time he yells
Gonna bring that take-off artist down

Kill, kill, kill, kill
Kill, kill, kill, kill, kill
Kill, kill, kill, kill, kill
Gonna bring that take-off artist down

Mobile Line Gonna Take Me Away From the Curse of the Bullfrog Blues

(Stampfel/Antonia)   There are many versions of "bullfrog blues" out there, but none quite like this one.

Did you ever take a trip, honey on the Mobile Line?
Hey lord mamamama, hey lord papapapa
Talkin' 'bout the Mobile Line
It's the road to ride
To ease your troubled mind

Can you see the engineer, picking on a mandolin?
Hey lord mamamama, hey lord papapapa
Talkin' bout a mandolin
Tokin' on a reefer
And drinking bathtub gin

Did you ever wake up with bullfrogs on your,
Bullfrogs on your, I mean mind?
Did you ever wake up with bullfrogs on your mind?
Tadpoles
 Swimming up and down your spine

Come along, pretty mama
We're gonna live in style, live in style
Hey lord mamamama, hey lord papapapa
Swear we're gonna live in style
Won't be no bullfrogs
For one hundred miles

Now the whistle is a-screamin'
And the pound wheel's rollin;
Rollin' round and round and round
Hey lord mama, hey lord papa
Rollin' round and round
And the whistle is a-screamin'
And howlin' like a lonesome hound

I ever return
Honey to this bullfrog town
Hey lord mama, hey lord papa

Talkin' 'bout the bullfrog town
Gonna take a gun and shoot all the people down

Well you think I'm evil
And evil is what I am
Hey lord mamamam, hey lord papapapa
Evil is what I am
I'm the evilest
Bullfrog-stomper in Alabam

I'm happy to escape
The power of the bullfrog, power of the bullfrog
Bullfrog curse
I'm happy to escape the
Power of the bullfrog curse
Cause the Mobile Line beats
Riding in a hearse.

"The Duji Song"
(Stampfel/Antonia)   As mixed by Mohawk, the lyrics are nearly indecipherable at times; this is my best effort. "Duji" is, of course, street slang for heroin, the melody recalls the smart-ass little parodies we all wrote and sang as kids, and Mohawk tosses in the chipmunk voices for good measure.

My ma gave me a nickel
To buy a pickle
I didn't buy a pickle
I bought some duji
Do do do do do duji
How I love duji
I love to do my duji
I do, do, do

I'd go down on a mummy
I'll be a commie
I'd rip off anybody
To get some duji
Do do do do do duji
How I love duji
I love to do my duji
I do, do do!

Griselda

(Antonia) Possibly the best song written by Antonia, and one of her personal favorites.

Come take a walk with me, Griselda
Wearing your dress that moonlight shines through
I am a sad and lonely boy
Since your mother said I couldn't see you

chorus
Slipping through the woods in the dark of the night
Calling to the moon up yonder
Oh lady moon, won't you shine your silver light
And lead me to my Griselda

Do you recall last night Griselda?
Learning the lessons nature taught us
Watching the fish jump in the lake
It was lovely 'til your mother caught us

(chorus)

Moonflower vine upon your window
Gives me a foothold for my climbing
I got a rowboat on the lake
Moon is out and all the stars are shining

(chorus)

I got a jug of wine, Griselda
Why should you waste your time in sorrow?
Hold out your hand and have no fear
If we're caught I'll marry you tomorrow

(chorus)

Jealous Daddy's Death Song

(Antonia/Presti) There are some who swear that Antonia has always been utterly obsessed with sex. This is a narrow and inadequate perspective on her. But it is not entirely wrong...

So now I'm leaving this world of sin;
One pretty woman with a lot of you men
I'm telling you boys:
Don't you monkey with my widow when I'm gone

I've had my life and I've had my fun
I've had more lovin' that you boys ever done
I'm telling you boys:
Don't you monkey with my widow when I'm gone

That girl was created just to be my bride
No other man can keep her satisfied
I'm telling you boys:
Don't you monkey with my widow when I'm gone

I know you can't wait until I'm dead
To try to drag her off to your waterbed
I'm telling you boys:
Don't you monkey with my widow when I'm gone

She'll just throw you out, and if she's feeling blue
She'll think about the times that I used to screw 'er
I'm telling you boys:
Don't you monkey with my widow when I'm gone

Well that girl's got class and a temper too
She can make a monkey out of all of you
I'm telling you boys:
Don't you monkey with my widow when I'm gone

And if any of you punks try to misbehave
I'll haunt your asses to an early grave
I'm telling you boys:
Don't you monkey with my widow when I'm gone

Bad Boy

*(Stampfel/Antonia)   A modern variation on "Stagolee," I was told it is not
about Weber.   But it could be.*

Mommy doesn't like him
Because he has long hair
Daddy doesn't like him:
He says he heard him swear
He's a bad boy
But I don't care

He knows illegal people
He does illegal things
He doesn't seem illegal
When he plays guitar and sings
He's a bad boy
But I don't care

chorus
Doesn't it kind of break your heart
Doesn't it make you sad
When the boy you love so dear
Turns out to be so bad?
He's a bad boy
But I don't care

Don't ever let a bad boy
Steal your heart away
You'll never get it back again
Until your dying day
He's a bad boy
But I don't care

He'll sell your heart on St. Mark's Place
In glassine envelopes
He'll cut it with a pig's heart
And burn the chumps and dopes
He's a bad boy
But I don't care

(chorus)

He's awfulness incarnate
He's wickedness on wheels
He'll ruin your reputation
How wonderful it feels!
He's a bad boy
But I don't care

He's Sodom and Gomorrah
And Cairo, Illinois
He makes it seem so boring
Going out with other boys
He's a bad boy
But I don't care

(chorus)

My life is so exciting
Since I'm going out with him
Romance is more romantic
When you know that it's a sin
He's a bad boy
But I don't care

(chorus)

Voodoo Queen Marie

(Antonia) This song is just flat-out wonderful, and it improves with each passing year.

Mother always said
Keep away from her
When she walks by the dogs all cry
But the cats all purr
She's a voodoo queen
Up from New Orleans
Here she comes now, looking like
The universe was all hers

Voodoo Queen Marie
She ran the town of New Orleans
Ever since her middle teens
Just like her favorite toy
That was fine because
That was just exactly what it was
Ain't nobody, ain't no laws
Made to fit Queen Marie

Has she got the power?
Don't the men all stare?
Golden hoops and rainbow clothes
Long black shiny hair
Hanging to her hips
Cherry-colored lips
Other women walk on the earth
This one sails through the air

Folks tell fabulous lies
They say the green light shines from her eyes
Say she's a cat in disguise
Say there's horns on her head
Say she's married as well
Say she married the devil in hell
Turned him into a big black snake
And keeps him under her bed

154

Watch that woman shake
Dancing with a snake
Dancing, dancing all night long
By the moonlit, candlelit voodoo lake
Dressed in flaming red
Dancing with the dead
Dancing all night long with a big red fish held
Over her head

Voodoos know her name
They pass the tales from hand to hand
You could pass all through this land
And never hear a word said
But if you know where to look
it won't be found in anyone's book
But the voodoos know and say:
Queen Marie is not dead

Synergy

(Stampfel/Antonia) In the early 70's Peter and Antonia were so completely in sync, musically and philosophically, that they could write songs and stories as a single entity. This one manages to mock spacey hippie optimism while affirming their very real belief in magic at the same time: a lot of meth and science fiction will do that...

Come along, sing with me
Sing a song of Synergy
Find that peace, in your soul
We're all one and heaven is our goal
Synergy will get us all
And its gonna be a ball
Kick that gong and ring that bell
Synergy will save us all from hell

Chorus
Superman's on the can, contemplating Synergy
Lone Ranger on the range and Doctor Strange got Synergy
Cool heads certainly agree concerning Synergy
Likewise Liberace's mama, Donald Duck and Dali Lama
Yessir!

Be a friend, lend a hand
Try your best to understand
We are all born alone
But the light of love will bring us home
We can have paradise
Right now at a bargain price
Heaven is ours to make
Peace on earth is there for us to take

(chorus)

Get undressed, plant a tree
Make love to machinery
Throw away all the locks
Open up the jails and stop the clocks
Eden's coming, Eden's key
Origin of Synergy
Magic and science, all for free
And a chance for all the kids to be

Dance in Slow Motion

(trad/Antonia) Set to the melody of a 19th century guitar standard that all young ladies of refinement learned to play...

Moonlight, wintertime chill
Here on the rooftop where everything's still
Stars spin, out on a spree
Dance in slow motion with me

Halftime, bottle of wine
You and the city both looking so fine
Hold my hand and you'll see
Dance in slow motion with me

Bridge
Here on the rooftop there's no-one around us
Only the moon and the stars to surround us
Here we can fly until morning light grounds us
Dance in slow motion with me

We could dance on the stars
Laugh at the cold and imagine guitars
Close your eyes and you'll see
Dance in slow motion with me

Jeanine's Dream
(Antonia) "Unplayed music will waste away" is one of the truths that motivated this collection...

In a trunk on the attic floor
The record lay 40 years or more
'til Jeanine came to poke about
In the attic she pulled it out
She decided to let it play
Unplayed music will waste away
So it spun on the old machine
It put her feet in a dancing dream
She was queen
Of the ball
Her surroundings fell away
And she danced in a carnival out of lost time

The record player was turned up loud
As she danced with a faerie crowd
A mean old grandma who lived next door
Heard the racket and called the law
The record player was still turned high
When the new rookie cop came by
Jeanine came dancing up to the door
She let him in then she danced some more
First he stared
As she danced
Then the music that was playing
Caught him in its spell and so he danced with her

Grandma came and she hollered "Stop!
Crazy music and crazy cop!"
But Jeanine didn't seem to hear
Then the music caught grandma's ear
She remembered those bygone days
And how she danced while the fiddle played
So she left them and went to bed
With the tune playing in her head
And she danced
In her dreams
With her husband one more time
And the record he had bought her spun 'til dawn

Surfer Angel

(Stampfel/Scherman/Antonia) A silly parody that sends up every teenage tragedy and surf song.

Sometimes the surf is pretty hairy
Told my baby it's too scary
Please don't take your surfboard out today
She told me "Don't be such a coward"
"God, you're such a sissy Howard"
Got to take my surfboard out today
She's hangin' ten across the Milky Way
I swear I'm going to ride with her someday

She hit her head on a hunk of coral
Left me searching for the moral
Surfer girl's a surfer angel now

My surfer girl was just fifteen
The blondest blonde you've ever seen
I taught her how to ride the roaring wave
I taught her not to fear the water
Was I doing what I ought
Or did I lead her to an early grave?

At midnight on the beach I sing my song
Darling wait for me it won't be long
My surfer girl was free and brave
She thought she'd found the perfect wave
But surfer girl is a surfer angel now

Random Violence

(McClean/Stampfel/Antonia) A chilling song, an hysterically-funny song. There are variant versions of the line "You may be barefoot, pregnant and poor," which does not rhyme. Antonia recalls a version that went "barefoot, pregnant and Gay" which not only rhymes, but makes sense in a nonsensical way.

I don't know you
But I'm gonna kill you
I'm sorry we're meeting this way
You are a stranger
But I'm even stranger
'Cause I'm gonna blow you away

Chorus
Random Violence, that is my name
Moral decay, that's what I blame
Ain't got no pity, ain't got no shame
I'm gonna blow you away

You may be famous
You may be fair
You may be righteous
I really don't care
You may be lucky
But this ain't your day
'Cause I'm gonna blow you away

(chorus)

You may be president
Potentate, Pope
I am psychotic
You haven't a hope
You may be barefoot
And pregnant and poor
But I'm gonna blow you away

(chorus)

Lonely Junkie

(Stampfel/Antonia) Some insist this song is about Weber, but it could be a half dozen other people who moved through the Rounder universe. Antonia tells me that she was thinking of Elvis Presley's voice and phrasing when she wrote it.

Ain't got no friends
They lock all their doors
Ain't got no buddies
Can't even get whores
Mom has disowned me
Daddy is dead
Ain't got no children
And I ain't got no bread
I got my monkey, I'm a junkie
Lonely junkie
Is my name

My bowels are in stasis
My atrophied ass
Is heavy and leaden
And bloated with gas
My past is a bummer
My future's a drag
I live for the moment
The moment is skag
I live for my monkey, I'm a junkie
Lonely junkie
Is my name

I'm locked in the bathroom
I just dropped my point
It fell in the toilet
They're closing this joint
But I got a good hit
So I really don't care
And I got my stash
And I ain't gonna share
I got my monkey, I'm a junkie
Lonely junkie
Is my name

Funny the First Time

(Stampfel/Scherman/Antonia) Just a silly ditty, kind of a relief after the last two.

When I was just a little boy
I hated rhubarb pie
I spit some at my daddy
And it dribbled down his tie
My mama laughed like crazy
So I spit some in her eye
She whupped me good and here's the reason why

Chorus
(Cause it was) Funny the first time
Funny the first time
It will never be funny again
So please don't repeat it
Cause I really don't need it
This big joke is coming to an end

Then one day I got married
Sure was lots of fun
I was her one-and-only
She was my only one
We ended in divorce court
After three months, maybe four
I don't believe I'll marry anymore

(chorus)

Now you may not believe me
But after I had died
I couldn't get to heaven
Cause I wasn't sanctified
And Satan says "who needs you
Messing up my nice clean hell?"
And as I was reborn they heard me yell

(chorus)

162

Low Down Dog

(Antonia/Weber/Remaily) This song has been much-performed by various incarnations of the Rounders and by others, with new and old verses coming and going merrily. The first four verses are Antonia's; the fifth was written by Weber and the sixth by Remaily.

Don't you take me for no low down dog (low down dog!)
Don't you know I got my pride, I just want to walk beside you baby
But you say, but you say
I must walk behind
Well I ain't holdin' still for none of that stuff!

Who will keep your bed warm when I'm gone? (when I'm gone!)
If you let the fire go out, better know what you're about my baby
But you say, but you say
"My bed's warm enough"
Well I ain't holdin' still for none of that stuff!

Who will mind the children when I'm gone? (when I'm gone!)
When you want to go away, who will take them out to play my baby?
But you say, but you say
"Kids are my whole life!"
Well I ain't holdin' still for none of that stuff!

Who will feed you peaches when I'm gone? (when I'm gone!)
You new lover may be cute, but will he bring home the fruit my baby?
But you say, but you say
"Peaches make me fat!"
Well I ain't holdin' still for none of that stuff!

Well don't you treat me like no Viet Cong (Viet Cong!)
Don't you know I'm from Danang; I just want to let it hang my baby
But you say, but you say
You gonna drop the bomb
Well we don't go along with none of that stuff!

Lotta wagons traveling down the road (down the road!)
Well you say I'm just one more, and that really is a bore
But you say, but you say
"My road's worn and rough"
Well I ain't holdin' still for none of that stuff!

When Things Come True

(Johnson/Antonia) One of many, many songs Antonia wrote with Mark Johnson, this was recorded by Peter Stampfel and the Bottlecaps as a gen-u-wine big rock & roll production number with kick drums and Maggie and Terre Roche and echoes of the E-Street Band.

When Things Come True!

It's like a dream, a place inside
Down deep in you, come back alive
Just when you thought all hope was gone
When things come true

When Things Come True!

You've seen it all, you're lost in space
Just then your life snaps into place
It's not a dream, you've found your place
When things come true

When Things Come True!

bridge
Doesn't the air smell good after the rain?
All these things I thought were lost
Are coming back again!

It's like a dream, a place inside
Down deep in you, comes back alive
Just when you thought all hope was gone
When things come true

When Things Come True!

You've seen it all, you're lost in space
Just then your life snaps into place
It's not a dream, you've found your place
When things come true

When Things Come True!

Fucking Sailors in Chinatown

(Antonia) A favorite of Antonia's, and also of many fans. Peter stopped performing this one for several years after two Chinese gentleman walked out of a show in protest, but it rejoined his repertoire by popular demand.

I am a Chinatown whore
I love the men I meet
My panties are lace, my head is spaced
I'm happy to walk the streets
And my favorite men are the sailors
I take them on for free
Cause there's something about a sea-faring man
That brings out the animal in me
When the boats hit the docks
Old Chinatown rocks
And my bed rolls like the sea

Chorus
Fucking sailors in Chinatown
Fucking sailors in Chinatown
Down in Chinatown fucking with the sailors
Ain't it a beautiful world

I can remember a time
I loved a sailor boy
His trousers were blue, his eyes were too
His tool was my pride and joy
But he was so young and so foolish
He wanted me for himself
I said "no good, cause my livelihood
Would rust if I kept it on the shelf"
So I cried for a day when his boat sailed away
And went back to my old self

(chorus)

New Happy Time

(Trad/Antonia) Antonia could write "straight traditional" with the best of 'em. This one would not be out of place in a 19th century southern hymnal.

When my life on earth is over and we've reached that final shore
There will be a joyous meeting with the ones who went before
There'll be endless glory and the sun will shine
Sing praises to our savior he has cast the demons out
Being in the good Lord's favor we will dance and sing and shout
Don't you know that there will be a happy time

Chorus
There will be a happy (be a happy time)
Blessed joy bells loudly (joy bells loudly chime)
From that happy moment to the end of time

There will be no war or sorrow when we reach that happy place
In that blessed bright tomorrow we will see our savior's face
Don't you know that there will be a happy time
In the wonder and the glory we will linger day by day
And the joyous angel music will banish cares away
Don't you know that there will be a happy time

(chorus)

And the Godless and the loveless who would not lend out a hand
Shall not enter into heaven, in the darkness they will stand
Far from glory where the sun will never shine
All the wickedness of ages it will not pursue us there
In his endless peaceful kingdom in his endless peaceful care
You can bet that there will be a happy time

(chorus)

Nightwalking

(Antonia) Both Speed Queens and Singing Bears need to prowl the streets at night...

Nightwalking, night winds are calling me
Through the streets, like a ghost in the land of the living
Circling the light, waiting for the night to end

Somewhere where the night pretends the darkness is a game
Neon lights keep shining in my eyes
Dancing 'neath the streetlight where the jukebox knows my name
Nothing could be realer than these lies

Nightwalking, I have no questions now
I have no answers, I have no need to answer you
Just a need to be walking quietly towards morning

Somewhere where the night pretends the darkness is a game
Neon lights keep shining in my eyes
Dancing 'neath the streetlight where the jukebox knows my name
Nothing could be realer than these lies

Nightwalking, I have no questions now
I have no answers, I have no need to answer you
Just a need to be walking quietly towards morning

New Limehouse Blues

(Trad/Antonia) Weber's ghost inhabits this one. Antonia has fond memories of her aunt singing the original version of "Limehouse Blues" while sitting on the piano at family gatherings.

Oh Limehouse kid, oh you old Limehouse kid
Going the way that the rest of them did
Poor broken blossom and nobody's child
Haunting and taunting, you're just kind of wild
Old Limehouse blues, got them bad Limehouse blues
Learned from the Chinese those sad China blues
Rings on your fingers and tears for your crown
That is the story of old Chinatown, Chinatown

Oh Limehouse kid, you've been pushing too hard
Trying to win but it ain't in the cards
Hoping for magic to take you away
Telling yourself you'll get straighter some day
Trying for China or maybe the moon
Spending your nights on the price of a spoon
Oceans of dreams where the dreamer can drown
Still hearing voices from old Chinatown, Chinatown

Oh Limehouse kid, where's the party tonight
What have you done now to get so uptight
Pasted-on smile that could dazzle the sun
Laughter so real it could fool anyone
Oh Limehouse blues, got them bad Limehouse blues
Can't put you down kid, I'm too much like you
That's why it scares me when I look around
and see that I'm walking towards old Chinatown, Chinatown

Places Where You Never See The Snow

(Trad Chinese melody/Antonia) Mating a mournful Chinese melody to a mournful – or is it? – tale...

I only see my uncle when the circus comes to town
Cause all year long he travels with the show, they come and go
He's fond of telling people he's a broken-hearted clown
But if his heart is sad you wouldn't know, it doesn't show
In fact he seems quite happy as he rides the circuit round
To places where you never see the snow

He likes to go to parties where the beer is flowing free
Always looking for some place to go, he's on the go
And maybe when I'm older he'll teach his tricks to me
Cause that's the only thing I want to know, I need to know
And maybe if I'm good he'll take me with him on that train
To places where you never see the snow

And now I am an old man looking back on happy years
My life has not been wasted this I know, I truly know
For though my father cursed me and my mother shed her tears
I left my home to join the circus show, I had to go
And I still hear the laughter of the children in my dreams
In places where you never see the snow

Laura the Horse

(Antonia/Stampfel) This is the kind of lyric that could keep a psychotherapist busy for a long time. Peter wrote the melody to capture the tone of Antonia's lyrics.

Laura's birth was human but a horse was in her mind
She couldn't be a girl too well, a horse was more her kind
You'd find her in the paddock at any time at all
And so they finally moved her in and put her in a stall
She had a friendly stable-boy and lots of things to eat
And sometimes lumps of sugar as a special Sunday treat
But the questions of her neighbors made her parents feel ashamed
There was fighting in the family and everyone got blamed

chorus
Everybody needs a dream, not many get to live one
Dreams are seldom what they seem so how much credence should you give one?

So they found a fancy doctor and they paid a fancy fee
And Laura nearly died from her enforced humanity
But another doctor saw her and he soon had it arranged
To move her to a stable where her parents never came
And there she lives quite happily, the stable fills her day
She dreams about her foalhood while she munches on her hay
But sometimes in her daydreams there's a green, unending road
And a silver cowboy rider and a saddle made of gold

(chorus)

Freddy's Blues

(Antonia) Freddy was a musician/dealer…

Midnight parts her curtains for me, following me around
Only to see me bump my head on morning
Where can I lay my love down?

Strange young girls come to my doorway
Trying their best to drown
Pulling them up I find that I am sinking
Where can I lay my love down?

Too much to say, nobody listening
Too little time, too much to do
Too many risks, someone's complaining
Well I don't mean to impose upon you

Here it comes, another evening; I gotta go downtown
Hundred and fifty people want to see me
Where can I lay my love down?
Where can I lay my love down?

Cajun Polka

(Antonia) Cajun and polka music careen into one another in a number of
Rounders songs, never more delightfully than here.

He came up from Cajun town looking for some action
Found a Polish bar there where polka's the attraction
Asked the band if he could try to play his fiddle with them
Though he was a Cajun he loved that polka rhythm

As he played a girl danced by, something seemed to start then
Golden-haired and blue-eyed, Helen won his heart then
In the break he spoke to her, when the dance was over
He walked her home in the moonlight and said please be my lover

She said: I'm a city girl, you are a backwoodsman
But I'll run away with you and do the best that I can
They set out for Cajun town, through the swamps at midnight
Pierre pulled the pirogue and Helen held the flashlight

"Wake up, wake up" cried Pierre, "Come out everybody!"
"Make my new bride welcome, we're going to have a party."
Helen showed the polka steps to the Cajun dance band
That is how the polka came to the Cajun swampland

Float Me Down Your Pipeline

(Antonia) I told Antonia that this one reminds me of a number of old Rounders songs, like "Halfa Mind" and "My Mind Capsized."

Float me down your pipeline, sometime
I came here with my guidebook, with my license in hand
But the landing field keeps slipping out of line
And this ain't what they told me I'd find

The biggest laugh around here is the changing ground here
Down in the alley when the game gets fast
Ain't no piece of paper gonna save your ass
So float me down your pipeline, sometime

I need to find a guideline, sometime
These old concentric circles keep spinning me out
And everything I do goes down in doubt
So won't you show me which way is out

I guess this is the moment when I might need a friend
Backwater waiting for my mind to break
Guess you're the only chance that's left to take
So float me down your pipeline, sometime

Delores on a Summer Night

(Antonia) This is a fitting song with which to finish the collection, because while it was never commercially recorded Antonia regards it as one of her finest. It celebrates teenage slutdom, a time in life that Antonia will likely always remember fondly as "the glory days." Like Antonia, Delores has no shame and no regrets.

Chorus
Put your love out in the street
Put your love out in the street
On this summer night so sweet

Delores on a summer night
Slips into her cut-off shorts
Strokes her green mascara on
And thinks a few hot summer thoughts
The street's a waiting mystery
There's action in McCarren Park
There's lots a teenage tramp can do
To keep it moving after dark

(chorus)

Delores cruising 'round the park
Streetlight shadows long and black
Three boys lean upon a car
Delores smiles and crawls in back
The boys take turns while two stand guard
Delores lights the night for them
The white-hot moment, deeply felt
They back into the night again

(chorus)

Delores on the basement stairs
Skirt hitched up around her waist
While the Spanish grocery boy
Explodes his way through his first taste
His youthful body moves her soul
Delores kneels to give him more
Aglow she takes, and gives him strength
She makes him whole, she makes him sure

(chorus)

Delores in her baby dolls
Dreaming in her narrow bed
Waits for sleep to come and rise
The quiet joy inside her head
The fire cool, but never out
The future stretches bright and clear
Delores thinks of summer nights
Blesses the fate that put her here

(chorus)

RESOURCES

The "Have Moicy" email distribution list is one of the primary ways that friends and fans of the Rounders stay in touch with one another: sign up at:
http://launch.groups.yahoo.com/group/have_moicy/

"Blue Navigator" is a Michael Hurley fanzine distributed from Ireland. The current issue is largely focused on Antonia. Subscribe at:
http://www.bluenavigator.net/

Mark Johnson, who co-wrote as many as fifty songs with Antonia, has a website: http://www.mark-johnson.com/

The Freak Mountain Ramblers are keeping the spirit of the Rounders/Clamtones alive in Oregon; visit them at:
http://www.freakmountain.com/

Corona, who contributed letters, songs, and good thoughts to this effort, has performed Antonia's songs for many years. She makes hats and sells 'em now: check them out at:
http://www.coronahats.net/

The live recordings of the Clamtones and West Coast Rounders can be ordered from Kathryn Frederick at:
http://www.jeffreyfrederick.com/

Maggie Roche has been an important friend to Antonia. She and her sisters, Terre and Suzzy, have made more wonderful recordings that you can shake a stick at and their tours are not to be missed:
http://www.roches.com/

Reach the editor at john.t.mcfadden@gmail.com

Also, please check out all the recordings referenced in the discography: most are in print in one form or another. Karen Dalton, mentioned often in these pages, was a true friend to Antonia and possibly the best interpreter of her music. She cut two albums before her untimely death: both have now been reissued as CDs.

Help keep Antonia's music alive!

www.ingramcontent.com/pod-product-compliance
Lightning Source LLC
Chambersburg PA
CBHW021012180626
46814CB00003B/1258

```
* 9 780615 137735 *
```